Loving Your Military Man

A Study for Women Based on Philippians 4:8.

Rejoice in the Lord always; again I will say, rejoice! Let your gentle spirit be known to all men. The Lord is near. Be anxious for nothing, but in everything by prayer and supplication with thanksgiving let your requests be made known to God. And the peace of God, which surpasses all comprehension, will guard your hearts and your minds in Christ Jesus. Finally, brethren, whatever is true, whatever is honorable, whatever is right, whatever is pure, whatever is lovely, whatever is of good repute, if there is any excellence and if anything worthy of praise, dwell on these things. The things you have learned and received and heard and seen in me, practice these things, and the God of peace will be with you.

—Philippians 4:4-9

Acknowledgments

To my husband, Jim, who has demonstrated Christ's love to me throughout our years together. Thank you for the fun, the adventures, and for forgiving me before forgiveness was even sought. Thank you for loving me with an everlasting love. May those who know us say we demonstrated Christ through our love for each other. I will forever go out on a L.Y.M.M. loving you, my military man.

Dave Boehi, editor, FamilyLife, thank you for your extreme patience in teaching, guiding and leading me as your apprentice. Thank you for editing each word, sentence, and idea I have sent you, but most importantly, thank you for your heart to reach military families.

Elizabeth Tyrrell, a wonderful friend, who has helped me countless times with her master skills of editing.

Amy and Bethany–two women who love their military men.

CONTENTS

Part I: Think On These Things

Part II: Think–Dwell–Also On These

Foreword

Welcome to this 10-week study of learning what God has to say about how to love a military man. Marriage, although a blessing, is not always easy. In the military culture a wife has to learn how to love, respect, and honor her husband even when he is gone for extended periods of time. This is even more essential when communication between them is limited and especially for when he returns from a dangerous assignment.

This study is intended to look at God's Word—primarily through Paul's book to the Philippians—guiding women into loving their husbands; beginning with their thought life. When times are difficult or stressful, she must rely on the truth of God's Word, memorize Scripture, and keep her mind focused on His promises. Her *attitude* is crucial.

This study is also intended to be a small-group experience—for women to share the joys and struggles they are experiencing in marriage. Each chapter includes an opening story followed by:

BASIC TRAINING:
Answer questions before group meeting (30-45 minutes).

ADVANCED TRAINING:
Questions to be completed within a small group (60 minutes)

MARCHING ORDERS:
Take home project (10 minutes)

ON THE HOME FRONT:
Questions to share with your husband
(to be completed before next group meeting; 20 minutes)

May God bless His Words and your hearts as you "think on these things." May He guide you with wisdom as you learn how to love your military man!

A word to group leaders:

Encourage your group members to complete the Basic Training section on their own before coming to the group meeting. Each group session includes some discussion about the individual time and then moves to a broader discussion of the chapter topic.

For the group sessions you will act as a *facilitator*, or discussion leader, rather than a teacher. The questions are designed for individuals in their group to freely participate. Be sure to lead the discussion by giving women who are normally quiet the opportunity to speak, and give everyone a chance to say something.

Encourage the group to speak of their husbands with positive, respectful attitudes. Don't allow the discussion to focus on negative or verbal assaults on men or marriage. Also, keep the discussion on target within each chapter; don't allow it to move in another direction for too long.

By reviewing each chapter ahead of time, you will have an idea how much time should be spent on each question (some questions will take longer than others to answer). Be sure to look up any Scripture references.

The study is intended to last no longer than two hours. Be sure to stick to the allotted time. Fellowship before and after the study is dependent on what the group decides. Be available if anyone wishes to stay after the designated timeframe to ask any further questions.

Familiarize yourself with the gospel presentation in Appendix A, in case you have someone who is a non-believer ask you for clarification on becoming a Christian.

Thank you for being obedient to God's calling in leading this study. May He guide your words each week, and bless you with His presence. May women come to know Jesus as Lord, and may marriages be healed as they learn how to grow in their love of Christ and loving their husbands.

CHAPTER ONE:
Oh Mom, I Want to Go Home …

Three days after Jim and I exchanged our wedding vows, bits of rice and confetti could still be found in our clothing from the well-wishers who bid us farewell at our wedding reception. Now I found myself sitting next to my Prince Charming on a hot, sweltering bus in Seoul, Korea. The strange sights and smells assaulted my senses. As I peered out the window, I saw what appeared to be chaotic driving, bicycles competing for road space, and mothers carrying babies in blankets wrapped around their backs.

There seemed to be no order around me in this place. The smells of garlic, cabbage—which I would later discover to be a favorite side dish called kimchee—and motor fuels, wafted in the air to create a mixture of strange odors unfamiliar to my young American nose. I wondered if I would become sick right then and there in front of my new husband and the hordes crammed together with us on the bus. Instead I swallowed my fear and focused my attention ahead.

I had given my life and my marriage to God at the altar, but I never knew how challenging this new life as a military wife would be.

This was the beginning of my life as a military wife. The few memories of our short honeymoon in Pennsylvania were quickly replaced by fear and trepidation at what would now be our new home. I had never been far away from my parent's home–let alone traveled to another country. Here I was starting married life with my new husband in a new country, wondering if this was really what "happily ever after" meant.

What had happened to my castle in the clouds? Instead, we would now be living in a dilapidated Quonset hut with no hot water. Our daily companions were mice and rats; we even began a game by keeping a penciled list on the back of the bathroom door of the number of mice we had each caught and eliminated. An encounter in our bedroom with a rat bigger than any rodent I had ever seen frightened me so much I had several sleepless nights. And showering with no hot water became an exercise in speed.

What happened to my prince and our evenings together in front of a glowing fire, sharing our love and talking of the future together? Instead, my prince would leave the next day to go into the field for maneuvers and would be gone an unspecified amount of time. The hours prior to him leaving were used for packing and saying our farewells. We had only been married five days and now we would be apart.

But that was only the beginning. One week later Prince Charming returned home with bandages wrapped around his eyes and head. He had been in a serious accident in a tank. The days following were filled with eye drops, burn cream, and waiting to see how much damage his eyes had suffered.

This was not what I thought marriage was going to be like. Prior to our wedding I had dreamed of the romance, drama, and the unknown of coming to this place. I anticipated the thrill and excitement of adventure. Now I found myself far from my friends, family, and everything that was familiar. I had given my life and my marriage to God at the altar, but I never knew how challenging this new life as a military wife would be.

BASIC TRAINING

(30-45 Minutes)

Answer the following questions individually before your group meeting.

1. What was your first year of marriage like? Briefly describe what was good about it and what was difficult.

____

____

____

____

____

2. How is your military marriage different than you imagined it might be?

____

____

____

____

____

3. What are some of the special challenges we face in trying to build a good marriage in the military?

____

____

____

____

4. How long did it take for you to realize the reality of marriage was completely different from your expectations?

5. Despite the challenges, there are also some wonderful benefits to a military marriage. What have you found to be *good* about being married to a military man?

6. If you could give one piece of advice to a woman getting married, what would you say?

A military marriage was not written on the pages of a fairy tale story– and it was not going to be easy.

I quickly realized a military marriage was not written on the pages of a fairy tale story—and it was not going to be easy. Your military marriage will not be easy, either. However, after 30-plus years of marriage—including 20 while Jim was on active duty and three overseas assignments—I can attest to the fact that marriage is an adventure filled with fun and fear, blessed by the sorrow of separations, and the joy of reunions. The question I had to ask myself was how could I distinguish between the fantasy I had dreamed about marriage and the reality of marriage? What could I do so the relationship, although not a fairy tale, would not become a "failing tale" instead?

In order to develop a more realistic view of marriage, I decided I needed to go back to the Bible for guidance. I wanted to not only gain understanding for my marriage, but also for my thought life, my prayer life, and for practical everyday living.

Why the Bible? Because the Bible has a lot to say about how we are to live our lives and find fulfillment in our marriages. One of my favorite books in the Bible—the New Testament letter to the Philippians—is full of practical ideas and direction for living.

ADVANCED TRAINING

(60 Minutes)

Answer the following questions in your group.

1. Let's start by sharing some of your thoughts from your personal questions found in the Basic Training section. How do you think a military marriage is different from a "typical" marriage?

What could I do so the relationship, although not a fairy tale, would not become a "failing tale" instead?

2. How would you summarize your first year of marriage?

3. What do you now know about marriage that you wish you knew prior to getting married—something that would have helped you to adjust to being a military wife?

Paul's Practical Training

In this study we're going to look at the book of Philippians, written by the apostle Paul—formerly known as Saul of Tarsus. Philippi was the first church established by Paul in Europe (Acts 16:12). Paul's intent in writing this letter to the Philippians was practical in nature, and he addressed several personal issues. Should you take the time to read the entire book of Philippians, his letter would be like reading a message from a friend. He sends words of gratitude for gifts sent to him during his imprisonment, addresses conflicts he has heard of in the church in Philippi, and throughout his letter gives direction on trusting their lives to Jesus regardless of the situations in which they find themselves.

If you had been in Philippi when this letter was received you would have been given the opportunity to read his pearls of wisdom firsthand. Although we are not living in Paul's day, his words are still as true today as they were when they were originally written.

Paul was known for persecuting followers of Christ until he experienced his own conversion to Christianity. Eventually Paul was imprisoned several times because of his belief in Christ.

In fact, Paul suffered through numerous trials during his years of ministry. He was beaten, stoned, shipwrecked, faced starvation, and encountered other physical sufferings. Yet in spite of all Paul endured, he still penned these words on rejoicing in every circumstance:

> *Rejoice in the Lord always; again I will say, rejoice! Let your gentle spirit be known to all men. The Lord is near. Be anxious for nothing, but in everything by prayer and supplication with thanksgiving let your requests be made known to God. And the peace of God, which surpasses all comprehension, will guard your hearts and your minds in Christ Jesus. Finally, brethren, whatever is true, whatever is honorable, whatever is right, whatever is pure,*

whatever is lovely, whatever is of good repute, if there is any excellence and if anything worthy of praise, dwell on these things. The things you have learned and received and heard and seen in me, practice these things, and the God of peace will be with you.

—Philippians 4:4-9

If you think about it, these are remarkable words. Paul is challenging us to think differently about our trials and our circumstances. He wants us to look at them with the right mindset.

As we focus our discussion on this one passage, we find several pieces of advice from Paul.

First Tidbit of Advice From Paul

Rejoice in the Lord always; again I will say, rejoice! Let your gentle spirit be known to all men. The Lord is near.

—Philippians 4:4-5

4. In this passage Paul exhorts the church at Philippi to rejoice. Paul regards rejoicing so important he uses the word "joy" or "rejoice" 16 times in Philippians. Why do you think he considers this so important—that we should rejoice in the Lord in spite of how we sometimes feel?

5. We've talked about some of the challenges of a military marriage. But what can we *rejoice* about in marriage? What can you rejoice specifically about in your husband?

6. According to Paul, we are to have gentleness in our attitude. How is this possible when we might face circumstances that are challenging in marriage?

Second Tidbit of Advice From Paul

Be anxious for nothing, but in everything by prayer and supplication with thanksgiving let your requests be made known to God. And the peace of God, which surpasses all comprehension, will guard your hearts and your minds in Christ Jesus.

—Philippians 4:6-7

7. Prayer expresses trust in God. Why is it essential to trust God with our marriage and husband?

8. What will having trust in God do for a relationship between a husband and wife?

Third Tidbit of Advice From Paul

Finally, brethren, whatever is true, whatever is honorable, whatever is right, whatever is pure, whatever is lovely, whatever is of good repute, if there is any excellence and if anything worthy of praise, dwell on these things.

—Philippians 4:8

9. What do you think it means to "let your mind dwell" on the things Paul includes in this verse—whatever is true, honorable, pure, lovely, etc.?

10. Of the eight positive thoughts Paul mentions, which do you struggle with the most when it comes to thinking about your circumstances or problems? If possible, give an example.

Fourth Tidbit of Advice From Paul

The things you have learned and received and heard and seen in me, practice these things, and the God of peace will be with you.

—Philippians 4:9

11. What do you think Paul means when he says we should practice "the things which you have learned and received and heard and seen in me"? How can we apply this exhortation?

12. Can you share a time when you "practiced" something from the Bible and the situation resulted in God's peace?

13. What is one new thing you learned from Paul's advice in Philippians 4:4-9? How do you think you can practice this principle at home in order to more effectively love your military husband?

If I had taken these tips of advice from Paul early on in my marriage, I might have avoided viewing my marriage as a fairy tale that might end as a "failing tale." I took a few years to learn how to look at my marriage with a different mindset—a biblical mindset.

MARCHING ORDERS

(10 minutes)

1. Do you understand what it means to rejoice ray with thanksgiving et your mind dwell on the best of things? If you answered "no" to any of these questions, stop now and ask God to open your heart to the changes you need to make in order to rejoice, think, and practice loving your husband. You may want to pray as follows:

   Father, thank you for never leaving me, even during the times I have not acknowledged you in my life. I ask you to forgive me. Please open my eyes and heart to what You want me to learn as I begin to study what it means to rejoice, to trust, and allow my mind to think of the things You desire. Show me where I can change my attitude toward my husband and my marriage. I pray this in Jesus name, amen.

2. Look at your calendar and find a time to schedule a date with your husband in order to share the husband/wife questions at the end of the chapter. Be sure to ask him to put the date night in his calendar.

3. Pray about your date night. Remember that your husband has not been in the study with you and he may not be ready to open up about marriage or spiritual issues. Be sensitive to what he wants to share and don't push him into answering any question. Begin by practicing what you have learned about rejoicing, trusting, and right thinking toward him.

   Also, be sure to let him know that you're participating in this study for *your* spiritual growth, *your* growth as a wife, and *your* understanding of marriage to a military man. You're not undertaking the study because you want him to change. Ask him if he is willing to answer a few questions pertaining to your study (promising to share only those things he gives you permission to share).

4. In preparation for the next eight chapters, memorize Philippians 4:8.

ON THE HOME FRONT

(20 minutes)

Discuss the following with your husband.

- Share with your husband (in a few sentences) what you have learned this past week in your small group. Perhaps you rediscovered what it means to rejoice or to think about what God asks us to think about. Or you may have recognized what it means to love your husband in a new way.

- What are some things we can rejoice about in our marriage?

- What one goal, as a couple, can help us begin exhibiting positive attitudes in our marriage and toward each other?

- What one thing would you like me to do differently in order to be more positive in my attitude toward our marriage?

- What is the best way I can show you I am supportive of your career? Is there something I can change?

Notes

Notes

CHAPTER TWO:
Whatever Is True

Do you remember the day you were married? You may have had a simple ceremony with only two friends as witnesses. Or maybe you had a large, elaborate wedding with guests arriving from all over the country.

Your idea of the perfect wedding probably included friends who would stand as bridesmaids, a father, brother, or some other male guardian who held your arm as you walked down the aisle, and a three-tier cake at your reception. No matter what the setting, who was invited, or who gave the blessing, a wedding day is a something you never forget.

That is certainly the case for Jim and me. We set our wedding date for mid-October in upstate New York, so we anticipated the autumnal colors of gold, yellow, and orange. Although those colors were beautifully arrayed among the trees on our wedding day, one thing we didn't expect was rain showers. This was not something I planned or imagined would happen, but it not only rained, it poured hard all day.

The struggle between negative thinking and what I knew to be true about my love for Jim lasted only for a moment.

What really jolted me to reality on this most momentous of occasions, was my father who held my arm at the entrance of the chapel. There we were—my prince only an aisle length away from me, the pews filled with friends and family, the organ beginning its wedding rendition. My dad leaned over and whispered ever so softly into my ear: "It isn't too late. If you have changed your mind, you can turn around right now and together we can walk out this door."

At this point several thoughts went through my mind. Perhaps my dad knew a lot more about marriage than I had given him credit for—after all, he and my mother had been married for more than 30 years. Although I knew my parents loved each other, I also knew their marriage was one of loneliness and isolation at times. Arguments between them were not uncommon in our home.

I also knew of other couples that had struggled with their marriages and had even pursued divorce. Were those the realities of marriage I should anticipate? Or did Jim and I have a better hope for our future? I wanted to believe those instances of discontent and unhappiness between other couples were just an anomaly. My dream and desire was to live happily ever after with this man who was about to be my husband. My hope was Jim and I would be the best of friends.

The struggle between negative thinking and what I knew to be true about my love for Jim lasted only for a moment. As I looked up the aisle and saw Jim standing there waiting for me I knew I wanted to be his wife. There was so much of this man I didn't know and still wanted to discover. So, in that brief moment, as my father whispered in my ear, I could either let my thoughts dwell on negative, insecure ideas, or I could let my mind dwell on what was true of Jim, our love, our union as husband and wife, and our future together. And then the music began …"Here comes the bride."

BASIC TRAINING

(30-45 Minutes)

Answer the following questions individually before your first meeting.

Words travel in circles in our minds. For example, we find ourselves replaying a song over and over in our thoughts until the words become so invasive that we try to avert our thinking in order to forget them. The same is true with the thoughts we allow our minds to dwell on. What is played over and over again in our minds can become like a broken record we can't seem to stop.

What is played over and over again in our minds can become like a broken record we can't seem to stop.

The moment my father posed his question at the entrance to the chapel, I realized what I allowed my mind to dwell on could ultimately change how I viewed my marriage. I could either dwell on what I knew to be true about our relationship and the foundation for our marriage, or I could slip into replaying my doubts, fears, and anxiety…things that often had no basis in truth. What I chose to dwell on then and in the future could make all the difference to my marriage.

1. What do you think would have happened if I had allowed myself to dwell only on negative thoughts about marriage on my wedding day? How would this have changed my attitude toward my marriage as a whole?

___

___

___

___

2. What are some expectations you had about marriage prior to your wedding day? Which expectations have turned out to be true, and which were false? How have you dealt with those expectations which turned out to be false?

3. Now that you've been married awhile, would you say you generally think in positive terms about your marriage and your husband, or in negative terms? Why?

When Paul tells us to "let your mind dwell on these things," he's not suggesting something for us to do periodically; it should be a continual exercise that ultimately affects our attitudes.

For the remainder of this study we will focus on Philippians 4:8, where Paul gives clear exhortation about our thought life:

Finally, brethren, whatever is true, whatever is honorable, whatever is right, whatever is pure, whatever is lovely, whatever is of good repute, if there is any excellence, and if anything is worthy of praise, let your mind dwell on these things.

—Philippians 4:8

To dwell means to linger over something (as with the mind or eyes). When Paul tells us to "let your mind dwell on these things," he's not suggesting something for us to do *periodically*, it should be a continual exercise that ultimately affects our attitudes.

In this chapter we will talk about our need to let our minds dwell on "whatever is true."

4. List at least three things you believe to be true about marriage. Why do you believe them to be true?

5. Now list at least three things you believe to be false about marriage.

6. In what ways would you benefit from letting your mind dwell on what is true in marriage rather than what is false?

7. Every person has positive qualities and negative qualities. Part of letting your mind dwell on what is true means acknowledging both. List at least four true, positive qualities about your spouse. How does thinking on the positive qualities change how you feel toward him?

When our thoughts are focused on what is true and positive about a particular person, situation, or event, our attitudes and actions immediately change. The tune playing in our minds will be one of pleasant, enjoyable words—replacing any repetitive, negative thoughts harmful to our minds and marriages.

ADVANCED TRAINING

(60 Minutes)

Answer the following questions in your group.

When our thoughts are focused on what is true and positive about a particular person, situation, or event, our attitudes and actions immediately change.

What we think is true is influenced by our upbringing, culture, and educational training. Media reports and television programming demonstrate how the world views the relationship between a husband and wife, which in turn influences our thinking.

This is especially the case with marriage. The things we think are true about marriage may be quite different from the truth we find in Scripture.

1. From your personal time, share your list of marriage expectations prior to your wedding day.

2. Now share the list you wrote of your husband's positive qualities from question 7 in your personal time.

3. Why do you think many people find it difficult to dwell on the positive rather than the negative?

4. As you think about your spouse or about your marriage, do you tend to let your mind dwell on positive or negative things?

5. What are some things our culture says are true of marriage? How do these things influence our thinking?

6. When we view movies or watch television, what type of attitudes or lessons do they seek to convey?

As we discuss what is true about marriage, it's important to pull back to a bigger picture. If our culture does not provide ultimate truth in such matters, where do we find it?

Who Is Truth?

We are introduced to the writer of Philippians, the Apostle Paul, in the Book of Acts. If you read through chapters eight and nine you see Paul's progression from an attitude of animosity toward believers of Christ to where he becomes a Christ follower.

Here is the description of Paul's encounter with Christ on the road to Damascus:

As he was traveling, it happened that he was approaching Damascus, and suddenly a light from heaven flashed around him; and he fell to the ground and heard a voice saying to him, "Saul, Saul, why are you persecuting Me?" And he said, "Who are You, Lord?" And He said, "I am Jesus whom you are persecuting, but get up and enter the city, and it will be told you what you must do." The men who traveled with him stood speechless, hearing the voice but seeing no one. Saul got up from the ground, and though his eyes were open, he could see nothing; and leading him by the hand, they brought him into Damascus.

—Acts 9:3-8

You see Paul's progression from an attitude of animosity toward believers of Christ to where he becomes a Christ follower.

The most important question Paul asks here is, "Who are You, Lord?" The answer was, "I am Jesus whom you are persecuting." Although Paul was persecuting Christians, Jesus made it very clear that Paul's actions were directed toward Him.

Who is this Jesus whom Paul is persecuting? Read what is written of how Jesus refers to Himself:

Jesus said to him, "I am the way, and the truth, and the life; no one comes to the Father but through Me."

—John 14:6

And the Word became flesh, and dwelt among us, and we saw His glory, glory as of the only begotten from the Father, full of grace and truth.

— John 1:14

7. Jesus says "I am … the truth." What difference can this truth about Jesus make in our lives? In our marriages?

____

____

____

____

Knowing Jesus as truth immediately poses another question:

Where Do I Discover His Truth?

The Book of Psalms in the Old Testament of the Bible is a compilation of praises, songs, laments, and sorrows written by various authors. These writers give insights into where we find what is true. Let's look at a few verses from Psalm 119—the longest psalm and chapter in the Bible.

> *I shall delight in Your statutes; I shall not forget Your word.*
>
> —Psalm 119:16

> *Your righteousness is an everlasting righteousness, and Your law is truth.*
>
> —Psalm 119:142

> *The sum of Your word is truth, and every one of Your righteous ordinances is everlasting.*
>
> —Psalm 119:160

The psalmist wants to communicate that truth is contained throughout the Bible.

Throughout this psalm, the writer uses various synonyms commandments, statutes, ordinances, and laws as references to God's Word—the Bible. The psalmist wants to communicate that truth is contained throughout the Bible. By knowing this we discover Jesus is truth, and truth is found in His Word.

8. How can reading the Bible every day help focus our thoughts on what is true, not only in marriage, but in all of life?

The Bible—God's Word—rings with truth from beginning to end. Throughout Scripture we learn truths about living, loving, marriage, and relationships. The best way to know exactly what the Bible says is to begin reading it every day in order to glean the truths we need.

Finally, in discussing "what is true" in the context of marriage, we need to ask:

What Are Some Foundational Truths in the Bible About Marriage?

Marriage was the first institution ordained by God!

Read the following verses found in the first book of the Bible—Genesis—about God's plan for marriage.

The man said, "This is now bone of my bones, and flesh of my flesh; she shall be called Woman, because she was taken out of Man."

Then the Lord God said, "It is not good for the man to be alone; I will make him a helper suitable for him."

—Genesis 2:18

So the Lord God caused a deep sleep to fall upon the man, and he slept; then He took one of his ribs and closed up the flesh at that place. The Lord God fashioned into a woman the rib which He had taken from the man, and brought her to the man. The man said, "This is now bone of my bones, and flesh of my flesh; she shall be called Woman, because she was taken out of Man." For this reason a man shall leave his father and his mother, and be joined to his wife; and they shall become one flesh. And the man and his wife were both naked and were not ashamed.

—Genesis 2:21-25

9. Why do you think God said it was "not good" for man to be alone?

10. When we marry we are, in effect, agreeing with God that it is not good for us to be alone—that we are better off and more complete with the husband God has provided. What are two or three ways in which you are better off married than in being alone?

11. What are some ways that you and your husband are stronger as a team than you are individually? What benefits does being a part of a team with your husband give you as a wife?

Adam and Eve had no one else to rely on but God to give them direction in this new relationship called marriage. They were instructed to leave, cleave, and become one flesh. It seems it didn't take long for them to adjust to this new union either. The next sentence sums it up nicely—they "were naked and were not ashamed" (Genesis 2:25).

Marriage is a Representation of Christ and the Church.

Read this beautiful picture of the relationship of Christ with His bride—the church:

> *Husbands, love your wives, just as Christ also loved the church and gave Himself up for her; that He might sanctify her, having cleansed her by the washing of water with the word, that He might present her glory, having no spot or wrinkle or any such thing, but that she should be holy and blameless … This mystery is great; but I am speaking with reference to Christ and the church. Nevertheless let each individual among you also love his own wife even as himself, and let the wife see to it that she respect her husband.*
>
> —Ephesians 5:25-27, 32-33

12. What would you say now is true about marriage that you might not have known before?

____

____

____

____

13. Is there something you have learned from this discussion about how God views marriage? If so, how does this change your thinking?

____

____

____

Marriage is ultimately the coming together of two individuals with their own unique backgrounds and personalities. In marriage we must rely on God for direction, recognize that God takes marriage seriously, and remember that marriage is a reflection to the world of the relationship between Christ and His church. We can move toward this goal by reading the Bible daily, focusing on the truths contained in it, and believing the biblical truths about marriage.

MARCHING ORDERS

(10 Minutes)

Take home project

1. Make two lists. In the first, list at least 10 things that are true and *positive* about your husband. In the second, list 10 things that are true and *positive* about being a military wife.

____________________	____________________
____________________	____________________
____________________	____________________
____________________	____________________
____________________	____________________
____________________	____________________
____________________	____________________
____________________	____________________
____________________	____________________
____________________	____________________

2. Check your family calendar to make a date with your husband to cover the husband/wife questions. Be sure to pray about your date night before you meet with him.

3. In our daily interactions it's easy for us to focus on the negative qualities of others and forget the true and positive qualities. Over the next weeks, begin to encourage your husband each day by telling him at least one of the positive, true items you listed about him. Words of affirmation are a way of honoring him and helping you to dwell on what is true.

Marriage is ultimately the coming together of two individuals with their own unique backgrounds and personalities.

ON THE HOME FRONT

(20 Minutes)

Discuss the following with your husband.

- Share what you learned from the study this week. Remember your husband was not a part of the discussion, so be sure to set the stage before you ask him any questions. You might want to tell him the study is focusing on Philippians 4:8, helping to steer your thoughts to what is true, honorable, right, pure, lovely, of good repute, praiseworthy, and excellent, and how that relates to marriage. He may want to know that this chapter covered the following topics: what is true, Jesus is truth, what is true is found in the Bible, and that there are many true principles about marriage found in the Bible. Two principles we talked about were: marriage is ordained by God, and marriage is a reflection of Christ and His church.

- What stands out in your mind about our wedding day? What is the funniest thing you remember? If we could have changed one thing we planned, what would you have chosen?

- Do you think I had a realistic idea of marriage on our wedding day? In what two ways was I not realistic?

- We are learning to exercise our thoughts by dwelling on what is true. Tell me two things you think are positive and true about our relationship with each other.

- In what ways has the military positively affected our marriage? Negatively? How can we change the negative in order to maintain a positive, realistic expectation of each other?

Notes

Notes

CHAPTER THREE:
Whatever is Honorable

I take this man to be my lawfully wedded husband. I solemnly promise, before God and these witnesses, that I will love, honor, and cherish him …

You could have heard a pin drop in the silence of the military chapel. We were now standing together at the altar, in front of the family and friends who had come to witness this joyful union of Jim and I—before God. My father held my arm firmly as we proceeded to the front of the sanctuary. Gently he laid my arm on that of my future husband.

Looking into my prince's eyes, I recognized this was the moment we had waited for and dreamed of during our past six months of separation. At last we spoke the words of the wedding vows, repeating after the chaplain.

If we had paused right then, I wonder if we could have honestly explained what these vows meant. Did we truly grasp we were standing before the presence of God and promising to love, honor, and cherish each other until death parted us? Did we realize God considered our actions at that moment as binding as the act of intimacy we would soon share?

When two become one before God in the presence of witnesses, the covenant is not only binding, it is complete.

After all, when two become one before God in the presence of witnesses, the covenant is not only binding, it is complete. Here we were presenting ourselves before the One who had given us the gift of each other, speaking words "to love, honor, and cherish," without grasping in totality the significance of their meaning.

I could not have imagined that soon after our vows were exchanged I would be questioning what it meant to honor my husband. Within a few weeks the honeymoon was over, the excitement of the marriage ceremony was fading, and the mundane of matrimony had settled in. I soon forgot the promise I made to honor the man God had given to me. How was I to honor my husband during the times I felt emotionally isolated from him? Honoring Jim was easy when I felt he understood my feelings and sympathized with my inadequacies as a military wife. But when his work became all-consuming, when lunch dates were forgotten, and when married life became tedious, honor seemed a vague notion.

The reality of honoring Jim was reliant on my emotions and not on the knowledge that God called me to honor him regardless of my feelings. Instead of honoring Jim I began to question his decisions, his actions, and sometimes even my love for him.

BASIC TRAINING

(30-45 Minutes)

Answer the following questions individually before your group meeting.

In the original Greek (the language in which the New Testament of the Bible was written), the term "honorable" means "worthy of respect" and refers to that which is noble and dignified.

A typical set of marriage vows might state:

> *I take this man to be my lawfully wedded husband. I solemnly promise, before God and these witnesses, that I will love, honor, and cherish him, and that, forsaking all others for him alone, I will perform unto him all the duties that a wife owes to her husband, until God, by death, shall separate us.*

1. Which of these concepts—to love, honor, cherish, forsake all others, etc.—do you think are the hardest to comprehend?

2. Which are the hardest to show when we least feel like it? Why?

3. Are the wedding vows "optional" in a marriage when things are difficult? Why or why not?

In our last chapter we looked at Paul's admonition in Philippians 4:8 to "let your mind dwell" on "whatever is true." In this chapter we'll examine what it means to let your mind dwell on "whatever is honorable." In the original Greek (the language in which the New Testament of the Bible was written), the term "honorable" means "worthy of respect" and refers to that which is noble and dignified.

4. What do you think it means to let your mind dwell on what is honorable?

5. What would be the opposite of honor? List at least 3-4 things. What happens if we allow our minds to dwell on them instead?

6. How would letting our mind dwell on honor help change our actions and attitudes?

When you let your mind dwell on something it will change your attitude. And that, in turn, will influence your actions.

Applying this concept to marriage is important. More than that, we need to know what it means to show honor to our husbands. Why? Because when you let your mind dwell on something it will change your attitude. And that, in turn, will influence your actions.

7. What do you think it means to honor your husband?

To "honor" means to "venerate" and "esteem." Honor shown to someone is a mark of respect and distinction. There are times when pride, hurt, and other issues prevent a wife from honoring her husband. However, God desires honor to be an ongoing attitude despite our feelings.

ADVANCED TRAINING

(60 Minutes)

Answer the following questions in your group.

1. From your personal time, how did you answer question 4? What does it mean to let your mind dwell on what is honorable?

God desires honor to be an ongoing attitude despite our feelings.

2. What do you think it means to honor your husband? Why is that sometimes difficult?

Demonstrating honor is a military concept. Honor is regarded as essential in showing support and respect to those who serve our country for freedom of democracy. In life and in death, the military honors its heroes for bravery and courage. Honor is displayed with medals, certificates, and ceremonies. Flags wave at half-mast, drape coffins, and remind us the honor due our country. Honor is shown when we hold our right hand over our hearts during the playing of the "Star-Spangled Banner."

In order to understand the concept of honor, a few questions need to be asked:

- Is it right to demand or to seek honor?
- Whom are we to honor?
- How does honor apply in marriage?

Should We Seek Honor?

Paul had reason to expect a certain amount of honor, veneration, respect, and esteem. After all, he was a man of status and influence. Paul explains his position to those in Philippi with this description of himself.

> *... although I myself might have confidence even in the flesh, if anyone else has a mind to put confidence in the flesh, I far more; circumcised the eighth day, of the nation of Israel, of the tribe of Benjamin, a Hebrew of Hebrews; as to the Law, a Pharisee; as to zeal, a persecutor of the church, as to the righteousness which is in the Law, found blameless.*
>
> —Philippians 3:4-6

Demonstrating honor is a military concept. Honor is regarded as essential in showing support and respect to those who serve our country for freedom of democracy.

Paul was not listing his credentials because he believed he deserved honor. To him, all this was nothing in comparison to his position as a Christ follower.

> *...whatever things were gain to me, those things I have counted as loss for the sake of Christ. More than that, I count all things to be loss in view of the surpassing value of knowing Christ Jesus my Lord, for whom I have suffered the loss of all things, and count them but rubbish in order that I may gain Christ ...*
>
> —Philippians 3:7-8

Here we find the man, Paul; intelligent, wealthy, of pure nationality, and a religious zealot; willing to forgo all of his accomplishments and status in order to know Christ and be satisfied with his position before Him. Because of Paul's humility, he was honored among his fellow believers.

Honor is not something we should seek. Paul told the Philippians that honor comes by knowing Christ and Him crucified, not by stature or position. When we reflect on what is honorable, and then when we show honor to someone, we should remember Christ's attitude about Himself:

> *Do nothing from selfishness or empty conceit, but with humility of mind regard one another as more important than yourselves; do not merely look out for your own personal interests, but also for the interests of others. Have this attitude in yourselves which was also in Christ Jesus, who, although He existed in the form of God, did not regard equality with God a thing to be grasped, but emptied Himself, taking the form of a bond-servant, and being made in the likeness of men. Being found in appearance as a man, He humbled Himself by becoming obedient to the point of death, even death on a cross.*
>
> —Philippians 2:3-8

Have this attitude in yourselves which was also in Christ Jesus, who, although He existed in the form of God, did not regard equality with God a thing to be grasped ...

3. How is having Christ's attitude a step to dwelling on what is honorable—especially about other people?

Whom Are We to Honor?

4. One of the 10 Commandments in the Old Testament is, "Honor your father and your mother, that your days may be prolonged in the land which the Lord your God gives you" (Exodus 20:12). What are some examples of how honor can be demonstrated to our parents?

3. Leviticus 19:32 tells us, "You shall rise up before the gray-headed, and honor the aged, and you shall revere your God; I am the Lord." Why do you think God wants us to honor the aged? How does this demonstrate a reverence toward God?

4. In Romans 12:10 we are exhorted to, "Be devoted to one another in brotherly love; give preference to one another in honor." What do you think it means to "give preference" to another person?

How Does Honor Apply to Marriage?

A woman who honors her husband totally accepts who he is, created by God, for her.

Honor and respect go hand-in-hand in demonstrating that we support our husbands. Honoring them shows we support what they do and who they want to become. A woman who honors her husband totally accepts who he is, created by God, for her.

5. Why do you think wives sometimes find it challenging to honor their husbands? (*Note of caution: Do not use this question as an opportunity to list negative qualities in your husband)

6. One way to honor your husband is to give him respect. Ephesians 5:33 tells us, " … and the wife must see to it that she respects her husband."

Why do you think husbands need our respect?

7. How effectively do you think you honor/respect your husband in public?

8. Another way to give your husband honor is to allow him to lead in your home. Ephesians 5:22-24 tells us:

Wives, be subject to your own husbands, as to the Lord. For the husband is the head of the wife, as Christ also is the head of the church, He Himself being the Savior of the body. But as the church is subject to Christ, so also the wives ought to be to their husbands in everything.

What practical ways can a wife allow her husband to lead in the home?

… as the church is subject to Christ, so also the wives ought to be to their husbands in everything.

9. Proverbs 21:9 states, *"It is better to live in a corner of a roof, than in a house shared with a contentious woman."*

What is a "contentious woman?" How is this opposite of a woman who honors her husband?

10. How should we apply the concept of honoring our husbands to our situation as military wives? How can we honor the choices he makes and the tasks he is called to perform?

11. What is one thing you learned in this discussion that you'd like to apply in your marriage?

Honor comes not from social status, intelligence, or who we are. It is an attitude that comes from recognizing our duty to give others preference and respect. It's important for us to recognize our need to honor our husbands even when our feelings dictate otherwise.

MARCHING ORDERS

(10 minutes)

1. To honor someone means to give high regard; to esteem. The best remedy for changing our hearts is to ask God to reveal where we are not demonstrating an honorable attitude. Once you have prayed, write yourself a note and place it where you will read it often (perhaps your Bible) as a reminder to honor your husband daily.

2. Make a date with your husband to go over the husband/wife questions. Pray about your time together before you meet. Begin honoring him even before he starts to share. Remember, we honor more with our actions than with our words.

3. Memorize Hebrews 13:4a: "Marriage is to be held in honor among all." We are to dwell on, meditate upon, think about, that which is honorable, remembering daily to honor our marriages, our husbands, and their jobs. This will help keep our minds focused on that which is true and honorable.

ON THE HOME FRONT

(20 Minutes)

Discuss the following with your husband.

- Tell your husband about what you learned in your study this week about dwelling on what is honorable. Share with him how we should never seek honor. Honor only comes from our standing with Christ. We are told in scripture to honor our parents, the aged, and marriage. Since "marriage is to be held in honor," you may want to tell him of your desire to honor not only him but your marriage as a whole.

- How effective am I in showing honor/respect to you?

____

____

____

____

- If I could do one thing at home to improve my honor/respect toward you, what would you suggest? In public?

- Do I demonstrate a respectful attitude to you regarding your military career? What could I do differently?

- What kind of impact has my level of respect had on you? Positive? Negative?

Notes

Notes

CHAPTER FOUR:
Whatever is Right

The marriage ceremony was over … the honeymoon a distant memory.

Jim was posted to Korea, and within 24 hours of our arrival he went "down range." A new bride, and yet I was alone. Alone with my thoughts, dreams, and memories of what I thought marriage was going to be. Like a princess, I would wait for my knight to ride back on his white steed and we would return to our romantic life together.

In the meantime, I reflected about all Jim and I had talked about before we married. We had spent hours sharing about our backgrounds and what life was like in our homes growing up.

We were raised in totally different environments. I had never lived outside of New York, where my father struggled in running a roofing and aluminum siding business. In my home we went to the grandparents home every week, weekend, and holiday.

Our parents had certain expectations of us in our behavior and response to authority.

Jim's father was a professional soldier, retiring after serving 30 years in the Army. Jim had moved many times in his young years. By the time Jim was in the sixth grade he had moved seven times. Jim's family would spend their holidays with friends instead of relatives.

As I sat thinking about our differences, I realized that as Jim and I moved into marriage, we had brought with us all our own personal histories, traditions, standards, and philosophies. How would we decide what traditions we would follow? Whose family would we visit when we were close to home? Where would we go to church? How would we decide to reconcile when we had differences? How would we raise our children?

In some ways, however, we had been raised with similar standards. Jim grew up attending church with his parents and five siblings in a conservative religious tradition. I, too, went to a traditional church, accompanied by my six siblings and mother. We were both taught right from wrong. Our parents had certain expectations of us in our behavior and response to authority. Punishment was issued for disobeying or making wrong choices.

But would we bring those same standards into our relationship and family? Or would we be tempted to choose the world's standards? Whether in the choice of places we would go, movies we would watch, or others we would spend time with, would we compromise what we knew to be right?

In fact, as the years went by we did compromise some of the standards we knew to be right. We made wrong choices individually and as a couple. And we began demanding our own way. The standards of forgiveness and reconciliation that we knew to be right were long forgotten.

If I could have looked into a crystal ball those early days of our marriage as I waited for my knight to return, and seen our future, it would have broken my heart. Our actions and attitudes, and our compromise in standards began a gradual unraveling of intimacy and love. If we could have only seen the breadth of unspoken distance that would open up between us, perhaps we could have prevented the breakdown of our once romantic marriage.

BASIC TRAINING

(30-45 Minutes)

Answer the following questions individually before your group meeting.

> *Finally, brethren, whatever is true, whatever is honorable, whatever is right, whatever is pure, whatever is lovely, whatever is of good repute, if there is any excellence and if anything worthy of praise, dwell on these things.*

Throughout this study we have been looking at Philippians 4:8.

In this chapter we will discuss dwelling on "whatever is right." Here, the word "right" means things that are "righteous." Paul was telling the Philippians to think according to God's righteous standards.

In the early years of our marriage, if Jim and I had ever stopped to assess our daily choices as a husband and wife against God's righteous standards, we would have realized we had fallen drastically short. God's righteousness is all encompassing. It includes thinking about things that are wholesome and healthy and making choices that are nourishing to our spiritual growth—being honest, forgiving others, keeping free of worldly influences, etc.

God's righteousness is all encompassing. It includes thinking about things that are wholesome and healthy and making choices that are nourishing to our spiritual growth ...

1. Living righteously means living according to moral standards. List some moral standards with which you were raised. How did those standards affect who you are today?

2. How were these standards different from those of your husband's?

3. What righteous, moral standards did you agree to bring into your marriage? In child-raising?

4. The world tells us there are no moral absolutes, no righteous standards with which to measure behavior. Can you think of some philosophies the world teaches which would be contrary to God's righteous standards?

5. How could dwelling on God's righteous standards affect our thinking?

6. The opposite of righteous thinking is unrighteous thinking. If we allow our minds to dwell on what is unrighteousness, what happens?

There was only one Man who ever lived a totally righteous life, and that was Jesus. We are called to become more and more Christ-like in our thinking and actions … and this is a direct result of dwelling on His righteousness. In order to build a godly home, with a foundation based on forgiveness, reconciliation, and right choices in everything we say and do, we need a standard of righteous thinking that will result in righteous living.

There was only one Man who ever lived a totally righteous life, and that was Jesus.

ADVANCED TRAINING

(60 Minutes)

1. Share with the group how you answered question 1 in your personal time. With what moral standards were you raised?

2. What are some examples of how God's righteous standards differ from those of the world's?

The Righteousness of Christ

Dwelling on what is "righteous" can be a difficult concept to understand. One way to clarify this is to observe the life of Jesus Christ.

Christ's standard of righteousness is also the model of how we are to live out our lives.

Paul wrote to the Philippians about his desire to "be found in Him, not having a righteousness of my own derived from the law, but that which is through faith in Christ, the righteousness which comes from God on the basis of faith" (Philippians 3:9). Not only does righteousness come through faith in God, but Christ's standard of righteousness is also the model of how we are to live out our lives. Jesus lived a perfect life of righteousness. All He did and said demonstrated God's righteousness toward mankind. He established how we are to live with our thoughts, words, and actions.

In the letter to the Ephesians, Paul admonishes those in Ephesus to adjust their thinking:

> *… and that you be renewed in the spirit of your mind, and put on the new self, which in the likeness of God has been created in righteousness and holiness of the truth.*
>
> —Ephesians 4:23-24

3. How would renewing our minds by dwelling on God's righteousness and holiness benefit our marriages?

4. Why is it difficult at times to focus our thoughts on God's righteousness when surrounded by unrighteous behavior?

Righteous Thinking Leads to Righteous Speaking

Righteous thinking is considering what is respectable, honorable, upright, and good. It is dwelling on Jesus' righteous life. When we are consistent in this effort, it will affect our speech and behavior.

5. Read Proverbs 10:31-32:

The mouth of the righteous flows with wisdom, but the perverted tongue will be cut out. The lips of the righteous bring forth what is acceptable, but the mouth of the wicked what is perverted.

What do you think it means for "wisdom" to flow out of the mouths of those who are righteous? What are some examples you've seen of someone who spoke with "wisdom" and of someone who spoke what was "perverted"?

6. Now read Ephesians 4:29:

Let no unwholesome word proceed from your mouth, but only such a word as is good for edification according to the need of the moment, that it may give grace to those who hear.

What do you think it means to "let no unwholesome word proceed from your mouth?"

7. How would you apply these concepts in the way you talk to your husband?

8. If you can, share an example of a time when you spoke in an *unedifying* way to your husband, and also of a time when you spoke in an *edifying* way.

9. Does responding with words which are righteous come easily? What advice would you give a woman who is having trouble talking in an acceptable way to her husband?

Words spoken in haste are generally words that are not edifying or righteous. Only words which build up another person; words of forgiveness and reconciliation, words which praise and not put down, are righteous.

Righteous Actions

10. Dwelling on what is righteous will not only affect our words, but also our actions. Read what Paul says in 4:31-32:

Let all bitterness and wrath and anger and clamor and slander be put away from you, along with all malice. And be kind to one another, tender-hearted, forgiving each other, just as God in Christ has also forgiven you.

What happens when bitterness, wrath, anger, clamor, or slander are part of your household?

11. Why is it essential to be kind or tenderhearted toward your husband?

12. Why is it essential to forgive one another "just as God in Christ has also forgiven you?"

Sometimes it is easier to act righteous—pretending we have all the answers and that we know what is best for others. The most difficult thing to do at times is to evaluate our own choices in light of God's standards of righteousness. Do we act as though we know what is right for everyone else? This question needs to be answered under the scrutiny of God's loving eyes. He reveals where we are falling short of righteousness in our actions and attitudes toward others.

In Philippians 1:9-11, Paul writes:

> *And this I pray that your love may abound still more and more, in real knowledge and all discernment, so that you may approve the things that are excellent, in order to be sincere and blameless until the day of Christ, having been filled with the fruit of righteousness which comes through Jesus Christ, to the glory and praise of God.*

Paul wanted his readers to understand that being filled with righteousness brought glory and praise to God. Responding righteously is a manifestation of that characteristic. When we dwell on what is righteous, we find responding righteously will be a natural result.

MARCHING ORDERS

(10 minutes)

Take home project

In the book of James we are told:

> *Therefore, confess your sins to one another and pray for one another, so that you may be healed. The effective prayer of a righteous man can accomplish much.*
>
> —James 5:16

1. Stop for a moment and confess to God any time you may have offended your husband. Write out anything God reveals.

2. Once we confess our sins of acting unrighteously, we are told to pray for one another. In fact, Paul says that the "effective prayer of a righteous man can accomplish much."

The result is healing. Praying for one another is thinking on those things that are right in God's sight. Stop again and pray for your spouse, thanking God for him, asking God for healing in your marriage. Once again write out anything God reveals.

____

____

____

Your prayer has great power as you seek to change your responses, your attitude, and your thinking. May your prayer of healing become a reality in your relationship with your husband.

3. Copy and memorize: "There is a way which seems right to a man, but its end is the way of death" (Proverbs 14:12). Remember … that which seems right to you is not always right!

4. Make a date with your husband to go over the husband/wife questions. Pray about your time together before you meet. Remind yourself you don't "need to be right." You only need to recognize the One whose ways are right.

Proverbs 24:26 says: "He kisses the lips who gives a right answer." Purchase a bag of chocolate "kisses." Place one on his pillow every night for a week. This is another reminder for you to think and to dwell on what is right.

ON THE HOME FRONT

(20 Minutes)

Discuss the following with your husband.

- Tell your husband what you learned this week about "dwelling on what is right." You learned that this means dwelling on God's righteous standards and treating each other according to them. By allowing God's Word to dwell in our thoughts, by seeing how Christ lived a righteous life, and praying for God's Spirit to guide us, we are able to speak and behave with His righteousness. Knowing this should compel us to assess the moral standards by which we are living, and consciously make choices according to God's righteous standard of living.

- What moral standards were you raised with that you would like to see passed on to our children? (Share two thoughts each)

- How do you think the standards you were raised with—both positive and negative—have influenced who you are today?

- What spiritual standards would we like to change in our family that we were not taught growing up?

- Can we agree to begin doing one thing to increase our spiritual growth as a couple/ family?

Notes

Notes

CHAPTER FIVE:
Whatever is Pure

The eye contact between Jim and me spoke volumes. What was shared in our glance over the candlelit dinner was something newlyweds only dream of. The look surpassed what might be labeled love—our feelings toward each other going much deeper—radiating pure and untainted. What was the secret of this rebirth of devotion?

Only months before, the path we had been on was a path of isolation, selfishness, and pride—each taking a toll on our relationship. Consider the time we were scheduled for a lunch date. Jim was working in the motor pool and I planned to pick him up at noon. From his office he could see our car and would join me when I arrived. Unfortunately, his focus was elsewhere and for over an hour I sat in the parking lot. My feelings escalated from sheer annoyance into rising anger. I couldn't go into his office to remind him of our date due to security reasons, and there were no cell phones. So I drove home. There would be no romantic gazes between us over a meal when we saw each other that evening!

... God had intervened in our relationship. God had opened our eyes to how selfish we had become.

We began to reach an impasse in our lives as husband and wife. In fact, our marriage became strained and nearly dissolved during times apart due to TDYs, field maneuvers, and other demands that caused a sense of individual self-sufficiency. I became convinced that whenever Jim went TDY or was deployed, he was actually enjoying our time apart. He seemed to have an easier time during our separations, while I stayed home analyzing every action prior to his departures. I wanted back our times of talking and discovering each other like when we dated. We had moved into a routine of isolation with unanswered questions and silence. Jim and I had unrealistic expectations of each other and when those expectations were not met, we had difficulty adjusting.

We still had moments when we disappointed each other … times when pride and selfishness would again rear their ugly heads. The night before this romantic meal we had to discuss some misunderstood words. But there was something different between us now. We knew it was because God had intervened in our relationship. God had opened our eyes to how selfish we had become. He helped me to recognize that Jim could not meet all of my expectations, spoken and unspoken. I learned only God can fill every need I had. God also revealed to Jim his patterns of behavior. He would become stubborn and refuse to talk. God showed us that we were falling into the habit of not communicating and not loving each other unconditionally. By showing us how we were failing in our marriage, He had revealed His love for us individually and as a couple.

BASIC TRAINING

(30-45 Minutes)

Answer the following questions individually before your group meeting.

Marriage is made up of routine days, endless chores, and sometimes misunderstood words.

Marriage is made up of routine days, endless chores, and sometimes misunderstood words. Going into marriage, we believe we won't experience isolation or lose the love we have for our spouse. But over time our love can turn into something different from the pure, unselfish kind we had anticipated. Instead it can become distorted by our own needs and desires. The other person's needs become secondary.

In this chapter we will discuss the admonition in Philippians 4:8 to let our minds dwell on what is "pure." Although thinking on what is pure can encompass many things such as holiness, virtuousness, or faithfulness, we will focus on what we mean when we speak of God's pure love.

1. How would you describe God's love? What makes it different from the love we are able to show to others?

2. Paul defines love in his letter to the Corinthian believers. This passage reads:

Love is patient, love is kind and is not jealous; love does not brag and is not arrogant, does not act unbecomingly

Love is patient, love is kind and is not jealous; love does not brag and is not arrogant, does not act unbecomingly; it does not seek its own, is not provoked, does not take into account a wrong suffered, does not rejoice in unrighteousness, but rejoices with the truth; bears all things, believes all things, hopes all things, endures all things … But now faith, hope, love, abide these three; but the greatest of these is love.

—1 Corinthians 13:4-7, 13

In what ways has God displayed these qualities toward you? For example, how has God been patient with you?

3. Why do you think Paul concludes with the statement, "So now faith, hope, and love abide, these three; but the greatest of these is love." Why is love the "greatest?"

4. What happens if you let your mind dwell on this type of love as described in 1 Corinthians 13?

Paul's letters reveal to his readers *how* and *who* they are to love. He shares how God's love in us is not just for those who love us—that would be easy. But, as Christ's example we are to love even those who do not love us.

Paul's description is in total contrast to the world's. Love, by the world's standard, is responding with our feelings, returning love only when we feel loved—even in the context of marriage.

ADVANCED TRAINING

(60 Minutes)

Answer the following questions with your group.

Paul was a man who spoke of God's pure love from firsthand knowledge and experience. He shared with others how they were to demonstrate God's love in the context of marriage, with other believers, and even those who were enemies. He invested in the lives of people throughout the region he lived, and proclaimed Christ's love to anyone who would listen.

Read how Paul expressed his love to his friends in Philippi:

> *For God is my witness, how I long for you all with the affection of Christ Jesus. And this I pray that your love may abound still more and more ...*
>
> —Philippians 1:8-9a

To Paul, love begins with Christ.

Agape love takes an active interest in the welfare of others, based on love as demonstrated by God. Agape love is not simply a feeling, but a way of life.

Defining God's Love

The Greek language has three words for love that distinguishes Christian love (*agape*) from passionate devotion (*eros*) and warm affection (*philia*). Many of the passages about God's love use the word "agape." Agape love takes an active interest in the welfare of others, based on love as demonstrated by God. Agape love is not simply a feeling, but a way of life.

1. Read these passages in which Paul speaks of God's pure, "agape" love:

For God so loved the world that He gave His only begotten son, that whoever believes in Him should not perish but have eternal life.

—John 3:16

Have this attitude in yourselves which was also in Christ Jesus, who, although he existed in the form of God, did not regard equality with God a thing to be grasped, but emptied Himself, taking the form of a servant, being made in the likeness of men. Being found in appearance as a man, He humbled himself by becoming obedient to the point of death, even death on a cross.

—Philippians 2:5-8

... and walk in love, just as Christ also loved you and gave Himself up for us, an offering and a sacrifice to God as a fragrant aroma.

—Ephesians 5:2

What do these passages tell us about how Christ loved us? What did He do to show that love?

2. What does His example show us about how we are to love others ... especially those whom we think don't deserve love?

Paul further defines love in the letter to the Corinthians (see "Basic Training" section). This passage, spoken at wedding ceremonies, sung at anniversaries, and known by even those not familiar with Scripture, reads:

> *Love is patient, love is kind and is not jealous; love does not brag and is not arrogant, does not act unbecomingly; it does not seek its own, is not provoked, does not take into account a wrong suffered, does not rejoice in unrighteousness, but rejoices with the truth; bears all things, believes all things, hopes all things, endures all things … But now faith, hope, love, abide these three; but the greatest of these is love.*
>
> —1 Corinthians 13:4-7, 13

3. How did you answer question 2 during your personal time of the study? In what ways has God displayed these qualities toward you?

____

____

____

____

4. Divide into two or three groups, and then divide the following Attributes of Love among the groups. Take a few minutes to complete the following chart:

ATTRIBUTES OF LOVE	WHAT DOES THIS MEAN?	OPPOSITE OF THIS TRAIT
Patience		
Kindness		
Does not brag		
Not arrogant		
Does not seek its own		
Does not take into account a wrong suffered		
Rejoices with the truth		
Bears all things		
Believes all things		
Hopes all things		
Endures all things		

5. After coming back together as a large group answer: Which of Paul's "Attributes of Love" do you find the easiest to demonstrate? Which are more difficult for you?

6. How could a wife use this Corinthians passage to make her marriage "other centered?"

Loving Your Husband

7. As you look at the list of "Attributes of Love" from 1 Corinthians 13, which of the traits would you like to adopt to exhibit love to your husband.

Paul's desire was for all who read his words of encouragement in Philippi to become like-minded—rejoicing with him in his suffering; sharing his love of Christ.

8. In another one of his epistles, Paul wrote about how we are to love one another with God's pure love:

So, as those who have been chosen of God, holy and beloved, put on a heart of compassion, kindness, humility, gentleness, and patience, bearing with one another and forgiving each other, whoever has a complaint against anyone, just as the Lord forgave you, so also should you. Beyond all these things put on love, which is the perfect bond of unity.

—Colossians 3:12-14

What are some attributes in this passage that you don't find in the passage from 1 Corinthians 13? List below. Then, for each attribute, discuss what this means in the context of marriage. For example, what does it mean to love your husband with compassion?

ATTRIBUTES OF LOVE	HOW CAN I SHOW THIS TYPE OF LOVE TO MY HUSBAND?

9. Paul's descriptions are in total contrast to the world's. Love, by the world's standard, is responding by our feelings, returning love only when we feel loved. The world never challenges us to love those who are unlovable.

Why do you think it's important to not depend on the "feelings" of love in a marriage?

10. Give some examples of times when it's important to demonstrate love to your husband even though you may not feel like it.

"... Maintaining the Same Love ..."

Pure thinking begins by knowing and accepting God's agape love, and pouring that love into someone else's life—especially our husband's.

Paul rejoiced knowing others understood his joy came from faith in Christ. He found comfort in difficult circumstances when he knew others shared in his faith. Paul's desire was for all who read his words of encouragement in Philippi to become like-minded—rejoicing with him in his suffering; sharing his love of Christ.

In Philippians 2:1-2 he writes:

Therefore if there is any encouragement in Christ, if there is any consolation of love, if there is any fellowship of the Spirit, if any affection and compassion, make my joy complete by being of the same mind, maintaining the same love, united in spirit, intent on one purpose.

11. How do you think you can be "of the same mind, maintaining the same love" in your marriage relationship?

12. The world tells us that marriage should be a "50/50 relationship." What is your understanding of this philosophy?

God's pure, agape love is not self-centered, but other-centered. It is not based on feelings, but is a response to God's love. We are called to love those who are our enemies, love those in the church, and love our spouse unconditionally.

However, the most important, and sometimes the most difficult to love, are the ones we live with on a daily basis. Those we are committed to and show our most selfish side to—our spouse and children.

13. Knowing all of this about God's pure love, why is it sometimes harder to love the ones we live with and are committed to?

In the opening story of this chapter, I shared how Jim and my marriage had shifted from isolation to renewal. God rebuilt our marriage by turning our focus on Him. We realized unless God was the center of our home, *we* ultimately became the center. No longer did we expect the other one to meet our every wish and desire. We now understood no human could accomplish this. Paul directs our thinking to that which is pure—telling us to live with a pure mind and heart, having motives that are innocent, and recognizing that pure motives flow from pure love. Pure thinking begins by knowing and accepting God's agape love, and pouring that love into someone else's life—especially our husband's.

MARCHING ORDERS

(10 minutes)

Take home project

1. We are exhorted to have a fervent love that comes from a pure heart, a good conscience, with sincere faith (1 Peter 1:22; 1 Timothy 1:5). Pure love is provided only through God's love in a marriage. We must desire to have Him as the center of our homes in order to represent a holy service of matrimony to the world. Spend the next few minutes in prayer. Ask God to show you where selfishness has begun to take root in your marriage. Seek His forgiveness for any pride or "me-ism" in your heart, and rely on Him to heal your marriage from the destruction of self-centeredness.

2. Make a date with your husband to cover the husband/wife questions. Pray about your time together in advance. Go with the prospect of discovering how God wants you to love your husband with His pure, untainted love.

3. Make dinner reservations for you and your husband at his favorite restaurant. Take the time to focus on each other—what your day/week has been like. Allow those around you to see the eye contact between you reflecting your love. Give glances that would make even newlyweds wonder what your "secret" is!

4. Memorize: "Blessed are the pure in heart for they shall see God" (Matthew 5:8).

NOTE: If your husband is currently deployed, write a love letter declaring your unconditional love.

ON THE HOME FRONT

(20 Minutes)

Discuss the following with your husband.

- Once again give your husband a synopsis of what you have learned this week. Explain that God desires a pure, untainted love in holy matrimony. We dwell on what is pure by recognizing pure love comes first by knowing God's agape love, loving others by accepting His love, and demonstrating His love by our actions and attitudes—even to the unlovely.

Perhaps you could share about the three types of love found in the Bible; agape, eros, and philia. Since the focus of this week's lesson was on God's agape love and 1 Corinthians 13, you could tell your husband about the different attributes of this love; patience, kindness, not arrogance, etc. If he is willing, you may even want to read Colossians 3:12-14 to him. Explain that only through God's love can a couple hope to have a pure love for each other.

- What do I do that demonstrates love to you?

- Can you describe to me what you think God's unconditional love is?

- How could we better show this type of love to each other?

- Are we willing to let God's love be the center of our marriage? What can we do to be more diligent in this endeavor? Think of one idea you agree on (perhaps praying together daily, doing a couples devotional, participating in an outreach program, etc).

- How can we begin to create daily boundaries around our marriage to maintain a pure love in His sight? Take time now to write out three steps you can take to set those boundaries.

- Creating boundaries around our marriage is even more important when we are apart. What steps can we take to achieve a hedge of protection around our marriage during separations?

Notes

Notes

CHAPTER SIX:
Whatever is Lovely

When I first met Jim, I saw that he had qualities I had never encountered in a man. I was impressed with his spiritual depth, his seriousness, and his intellect. We talked about our religious backgrounds and seemed to connect on an emotional level I had never known before. I also found him to be the most attractive man I had ever met.

But as we began experiencing isolation and frustration in our marriage, I found that, to my surprise, the qualities that once seemed so attractive to me now became negatives. His seriousness drove me crazy. His spiritual insights made me feel as though I was in church every day. When he talked about spiritual things it seemed as if I was living with a "sermon in a cereal box"—they came every morning with a lot of snap, crackle, and pop.

... my introverted prince needed his peace and quiet, while his extroverted princess needed entertainment and fun.

The same switch occurred with the way Jim began to view my qualities. Initially he was drawn to my gregarious nature, my laughter, and my spontaneity. But at some point my spontaneity sent him over the edge. For some reason, he no longer seemed enamored by my jokes and antics—he didn't think throwing ice water into his hot shower was a cute jest by his jester of a wife. He didn't understand why I wanted to hold dinner parties so often—my introverted prince needed his peace and quiet, while his extroverted princess needed entertainment and fun.

We were two totally different people, who had once been attracted by our differences. Now those differences drove us mad with frustration.

Eventually, God revealed our selfishness to us and softened the rough edges of our natures. God opened my eyes to realize Jim needed quiet times in order to refresh himself and have energy to face a new day. Jim recognized my need for others and how I energize by interaction. We had to compromise in many other ways in our relationship.

Ironically, over the years we have become more and more like each other. I am at peace with having quietness in our home, and Jim is willing to listen to my jokes, perhaps still learning to appreciate some of my antics.

I am thankful God has given me laughter and impulsiveness, but realize those qualities could be more tempered with Jim's seriousness. I appreciate spontaneity but need Jim's calm deliberation. I am grateful for how Jim completes me with his character. His personality has rubbed off on mine, and mine onto his. One of the greatest compliments I have ever received was when our daughter stated how much I had become like her father. After all, that is what marriage is intended to be—two totally different people living, loving, and being one flesh. But, more importantly, our marriage is a reflection of what happens in our relationship with God. The more time we spend with Him the more we know Him, and the more we become like Him.

BASIC TRAINING

(30-45 Minutes)

Answer the following questions individually before your group meeting.

1. What qualities in your spouse first attracted you to him?

2. What one quality in your husband do you appreciate the most? Why is this quality important to you?

3. What quality in your husband that you originally found attractive is now sometimes irritating?

... our marriage is a reflection of what happens in our relationship with God. The more time we spend with Him, the more we know Him, the more we become like Him.

4. In what ways are you and your spouse different?

In this study we have talked about letting our minds dwell on what is true, honorable, right, and pure, as explained in Philippians 4:8. In this chapter we will be discussing the importance of letting our minds dwell on what is "lovely." This term means to be pleasing, amiable, kind, and gracious. The only time the word "lovely" is used in the New Testament is in this sentence.

The only time the word "lovely" is used in the New Testament is in this sentence.

When we meet couples who display pleasing, kind, and gracious qualities in their marriages we are drawn to spend time with them. We are compelled to be with them because we desire to learn how we can develop the trait of being lovely toward one another … despite whatever differences they have in personality and in behavior.

On the other hand, we have all seen couples who have appeared unlovely in their actions toward each other and their children. Their behavior causes us to be embarrassed and uncomfortable. When we see them we become aware of how unattractive some behavior truly is.

5. What is an example of a couple who you enjoy spending time with because of the "lovely" attitude they display toward life and toward each other? What do they do for each other to show a "lovely" attitude?

____

____

____

6. What one way could you begin to emulate this behavior in your own marriage? What could this potentially do for your relationship with your husband?

____

____

____

____

ADVANCED TRAINING

(60 Minutes)

Answer the following questions with your group.

1. Share your answer from your personal time about the qualities that initially attracted you to your husband.

2. What are some ways you and your husband are different? How do these differences complement each other?

3. Do your differences cause unlovely behavior between you at times? How and why?

No matter how well your personality and temperaments complement those of your husband, you will inevitably experience conflict in marriage because you are different from each other. But as we walk with Christ, there are certain qualities that He seeks to build into our lives that help us establish a strong marriage despite those differences. One quality is to become lovely.

I'm not talking about external loveliness in the sense of physical appearance. This is not the lovely that comes from correct posture, beautiful clothes, or perfect make-up. Instead, we are to be conformed internally in order to show the world His love by being lovely women and wives.

Becoming lovely is not necessarily something that comes easily or instantaneously. You become lovely by establishing a strong relationship with the Lord.

Becoming Lovely: Spend Time Studying God's Word

4. Psalm 119:11 says, "Your word I have treasured in my heart, that I may not sin against You." What methods have you discovered that help you to study God's Word? How have these been effective in your life?

5. In what ways can studying God's Word change your actions from unlovely to lovely? If you can, describe a time when God's Word influenced your behavior.

6. How would spending time reading the Bible help you accept your husband even when *he* isn't acting lovely?

Becoming Lovely: Spend Time in Prayer

Paul knew firsthand the power of prayer. His day-to-day life as a missionary was dependent upon his willingness to pray. Others would watch and be forever influenced by the power of his prayers. Acts 16:25, for example, describes what happened when Paul and his companions were imprisoned in Philippi:

> *… But about midnight Paul and Silas were praying and singing hymns of praise to God, and the prisoners were listening to them …*

7. Read Philippians 4:6, written during Paul's second imprisonment:

   Be anxious for nothing, but in everything by prayer and supplication with thanksgiving let your requests be made known to God.

   How does prayer influence our thinking? How does it make us lovelier?

8. Have you ever experienced a time when praying redirected your attitude toward behaving in a lovely manner to your husband—when at first you might have wanted to "get even with him?" Describe what happened.

Becoming Lovely: Spend Time With Other Believers

9. Read Hebrews 10:24-25:

… and let us consider how to stimulate one another to love and good deeds, not forsaking our own assembling together, as is the habit of some, but encouraging one another; and all the more as you see the day drawing near.

How can spending time with other believers, who are lovely in their actions and attitudes, help us become more lovely?

10. When you observe couples who display lovely behavior toward each other, how do you think they deal with their differences?

11. What are some examples of times when you find it difficult to be lovely toward your husband? How could you replace that tendency with a lovely attitude?

12. What kind of impact do you think changing this behavior might have in your relationship with your husband?

The quality of being lovely is not exclusive to the attractive or the wealthy. This attribute is for all women no matter their social standing, size, height, or personality. Oswald Chambers wrote: "We become like the person we spend the most time with, therefore, spend more time with Christ." Develop times for Bible reading and prayer and spend time with others who model a lovely marriage. We can only change by God's influence in our lives, His Spirit in our actions, and His lovely heart working through us.

MARCHING ORDERS

(10 Minutes)

1. What is the most important thing you learned from this chapter and group discussion? Pray and ask God to help you this week to begin implementing this change in your life. Be specific.

2. This is a gentle reminder. Have you memorized Philippians 4:8? The only way to externally display God's loveliness is by internalizing His truth. Begin now to memorize this passage if you haven't already done so.

3. Don't forget to make a date with your husband. Perhaps you could have a romantic rendezvous in your home after the children are asleep.

ON THE HOME FRONT

(20 Minutes)

Discuss the following with your husband.

Tell your husband what you learned in the study this week about what is "lovely." We learned that the term "lovely" means pleasing, amiable, kind, and gracious—graciousness that wins and charms. The only time the term is used in the New Testament is in Philippians 4:8. We discovered that in order to become lovely we needed to spend time dwelling on God's Word, spend time with God in prayer, and spend time with other couples who exhibit this type of love in their marriage relationships.

- Can you think of someone who demonstrated this type of lovely behavior—being kind and gracious—to you as a child? What did they do that makes you remember them?

- Is there someone who comes to mind who has demonstrated loveliness to you as an adult? What traits would you like to emulate? Why?

- Share three lovely qualities about your spouse.

- Why do you appreciate these particular qualities?

Notes

CHAPTER SEVEN:
Whatever is of Good Repute

As a new bride, I wanted to be the perfect military wife. I wanted my behavior and actions to be a good influence on Jim's career.

Where could I begin to learn about how to be a military wife? My mother-in-law, a military wife for 30 years, had given me a book entitled, *The Officer's Wife's Guide to Etiquette.* However, I felt overwhelmed with this step-by-step guide of what to wear and how to behave. So I shoved the book in the bottom of my dresser drawer.

My mother-in-law realized how awkward I felt as a new bride. So she decided to take me on a mini-shopping trip for appropriate clothing. Perhaps she thought the bell-bottom pants, tube-top, and platform shoes that I wore for our first meeting were not proper future daughter-in-law attire! So off we went on a shopping spree. Pastel pantsuits, cream blouses, low-heeled shoes with cute little buckles soon took their place in my closet.

... all I wanted to do was run home, put on my favorite sweatsuit, eat chocolate bonbons, and wallow in self-pity.

The day finally arrived when I would attend my first morning tea hosted by the commander's wife. I had my hair done, donned my best pantsuit, put on my make-up, and headed off to meet the other unit wives. As I looked in the mirror one last time I felt as if someone else was staring back at me. Who was this "new" woman and would the other women she met like her? Or was I going into a *Stepford Wives* setting where an attempt would be made to transform me into a clone?

I soon found myself sitting among the other women. Each of us had dainty china cups and small dishes holding finger sandwiches, setting precariously on our knees. At that moment I felt like anything but a lady. If my fingers had been any clumsier I knew I would find myself covered in tea and cucumber sandwiches.

Having grown up in a home where my father was a laborer by trade, I was used to CorningWare™ and chipped coffee mugs. I felt as out of place as Shrek at a beauty pageant! My clothing was uncomfortable and my new hairdo fell limply around my face. Each time I opened my mouth I lost my words, or felt I said some something offensive, causing each woman to stare at me in disapproval. At that point I realized I was no *Stepford* wife!

Instead, all I wanted to do was run home, put on my favorite sweatsuit, eat chocolate bonbons, and wallow in self-pity. I was back to feeling like a little girl in dress-up clothes. Was I destined to forever feel inadequate and out of place as Jim's wife? Perhaps I had a lot more to learn about what a wife was supposed to be. Maybe another glance at the book shoved in my dresser drawer might give me the answers.

Or maybe I was looking in all the wrong places to learn what I needed to know about being a wife—whether my husband was in the military or any other career.

BASIC TRAINING

Personal Time

(30-45 Minutes)

Answer the following questions individually before your group meeting.

As wives, we long to adapt to each new situation and assignment with ease. We want to demonstrate our abilities in maintaining continuity in our homes, even though each time we move we have to discover new friends, jobs, hairdressers, doctors, grocery stores, schools, and other crucial places. We want our husbands to be accepted, we want to feel comfortable in each new place, and we want our behavior and actions to be a good influence on those around us. And if a wife is on active duty, she wants all of these things to be a reality for her, too.

Each of the qualities Paul directs us to think about—"whatever it true, whatever is honorable, whatever is pure, whatever is right, whatever is lovely, whatever is of good repute…"—tie closely in to one another. Paul adds each new word like an orchestra reaching a crescendo, with each word resembling an instrument making a complete song when played together.

In this chapter we will be covering Paul's suggestion in Philippians 4:8 to dwell on "whatever is of good repute." The words are also translated "good report"—something or someone that is highly regarded or well thought of. Reputable behavior includes admirable qualities such as kindness, courtesy, and respect for others.

As wives, we long to adapt to each new situation and assignment with ease.

1. What qualities do you find admirable in other women? What traits, along with kindness, courtesy, and respect, would give a woman a good reputation?

____

____

____

____

____

Behavior affects a person's reputation. If we think someone acts admirably, it might be because they are known for not lying at work or maybe it is because they help others. Their behavior is a good report.

2. Why is reputation important in a military career? As a military wife?

____

____

____

____

____

3. How could a negative reputation harm others?

____

____

____

____

____

Although we could focus on many aspects of what reputable behavior might be, we will look at how God views a woman of reputable character by how she thinks and acts. We will discuss how a woman's thoughts and actions affect her reputation—the good or bad report others have of her.

God views a woman of reputable character by how she thinks and acts.

During the past several chapters we have discussed how our thoughts directly influence our behavior. Our actions, in turn, have an essential effect on our reputation.

ADVANCED TRAINING

Group Interaction Time

(60 Minutes)

Answer the following questions in your group.

1. Share your answers from the first three questions of the individual time:

   What qualities do you find admirable in other women?

   ___

   ___

   ___

   Why do you think these qualities are important in a woman?

   ___

   ___

   ___

   How can one's behavior influence her reputation?

   ___

   ___

   ___

In Philippians 4:8, the apostle Paul urges us to let our minds dwell on "whatever is of good repute." One way to have a clearer understanding of how a woman is viewed with a good repute, where thoughts and behavior are exemplary, is by looking at the woman described in Proverbs 31. Here we find a distinct checklist of admirable qualities to emulate. The external manifestations of her behavior are a direct result of her internal heart attitude.

The external manifestations of her behavior are a direct result of her internal heart attitude.

Read this passage from Proverbs 31:10-31:

An excellent wife, who can find? For her worth is far above jewels. The heart of her husband trusts in her, and he will have no lack of gain. She does him good and not evil all the days of her life. She looks for wool and flax and works with her hands in delight. She is like merchant ships; she brings her food from afar. She rises also while it is still night and gives food to her household and portions to her maidens. She considers a field and buys it; from her earnings she plants a vineyard. She girds herself with strength and makes her arms strong. She senses that her gain is good; her lamp does not go out at night. She stretches out her hands to the distaff, and her hands grasp the spindle. She extends her hand to the poor, and she stretches out her hands to the needy. She is not afraid of the snow for her household, for all her household are clothed with scarlet. She makes coverings for herself; her clothing is fine linen and purple. Her husband is known in the gates, when he sits among the elders of the land. She makes linen garments and sells them, and supplies belts to the tradesmen. Strength and dignity are her clothing, and she smiles at the future. She opens her mouth in wisdom, and the teaching of kindness is on her tongue. She looks well to the ways of her household, and does not eat the bread of idleness. Her children rise up and bless her; her husband also, and he praises her, saying: "Many daughters have done nobly, but you excel them all." Charm is deceitful and beauty is vain, but a woman who fears the Lord, she shall be praised. Give her the product of her hands, and let her works praise her in the gates.

Strength and dignity are her clothing, and she smiles at the future.

Many women feel overwhelmed when they read this passage—they're amazed by the amount of work this woman accomplishes, the laundry list of activities she is involved in, and how flawlessly she appears to accomplish her tasks. What is important, however, is her *conduct.* She is praised by her husband, her children, and for her works.

2. Verse 30 states " … a woman who fears the Lord is to be praised." This does not mean she was afraid of God, but was in a state of awe and wonder of who He is and what He had done in her life. Why would a woman who fears the Lord be praised and why is this instruction so important for us as women?

3. What are some character qualities found in this woman?

The conduct of the Proverbs 31 woman can be broken down into three categories:

- How she thinks
- How she talks
- How she acts

... a woman who fears the Lord is to be praised

How She Thinks

4. Proverbs 31:25 says, "Strength and dignity are her clothing, and she smiles at the future."

   Describe a woman you admire who demonstrates the qualities of strength and dignity. What actions demonstrate these qualities?

5. How is the ability to "smile at the future" important as a military wife/member?

How She Talks

6. What we think affects how we speak. Proverbs 31:26 states, "She opens her mouth in wisdom, and the teaching of kindness is on her tongue."

   How can a woman be sure that when she opens her mouth she speaks with wisdom and kindness? How would that affect how others view her?

7. Have you seen other women speak without kindness? Without wisdom? What was your impression? How do you think speaking unkindly can affect one's reputation?

8. What we think and say as wives can either build up or undermine our husband's good standing with others. How can this affect him both personally and professionally?

How can a woman be sure that when she opens her mouth she speaks with wisdom and kindness?

How She Acts

9. The Proverbs woman is praised because of her fear of the Lord. She is also praised by her husband and children. Read Proverbs 31:10-12:

An excellent wife who can find? For her worth is far above jewels. The heart of her husband trusts in her, and he will have no lack of gain. She does him good and not evil all the days of her life.

According to these verses, what qualities would cause a husband to praise his wife?

Our reputation is not simply about how others view us, but how others view God. He is relying on us to reflect Him to the world with our behavior

10. Why would trust be classified as an excellent quality in a wife?

11. How does a wife help her husband trust her?

12. Does trust establish a good reputation? Describe someone you know who has a reputation of being trustworthy.

13. How does a wife do "good" by her behavior so that her husband will have no lack of gain? How does she do him evil?

Our reputation is not simply about how others view us, but how others view God. He is relying on us to reflect Him to the world with our behavior. Knowing He is relying on us, and knowing our reputation precedes us as we move from one duty station to the next, should make us aware of the importance of our thoughts, words, and actions.

MARCHING ORDERS

(10 minutes)

Take Home Project

1. Over the next few days, assess your relationship with God. Can you honestly state that you fear the Lord? Would others give you this compliment? Make a list of what you can do to develop a healthy "fear of the Lord." These might include a more disciplined quiet time, prayer life, and time with other believers.

2. Make a date with your husband to go over the husband/wife questions. Pray before your time together.

3. Memorize Proverbs 31:10-12. One of the greatest gifts to give your husband is a heart of trust.

ON THE HOME FRONT

(20 Minutes)

Discuss the following with your husband.

- As you meet with your husband, explain to him your understanding of what a good repute would be according to God's standards. This might include some of the qualities you learned about the Proverbs woman—how she was praised by her children, husband, and for her work, but most importantly because she fears the Lord. Her conduct was admirable because her thoughts, words, and actions were all based on her relationship to God.

- What qualities do you think others find admirable in me? In you?

- Share two qualities you find admirable in your spouse. Add other qualities from the first question.

- What do you think our reputation is as a couple?

- How can we act in order to reflect God's reputation of love and respect? Do we need to change some bad habits in order to more effectively reflect Him?

Notes

CHAPTER EIGHT:
If Anything is Excellent

Excellence is an art won by training and habituation. We do not act rightly because we have virtue or excellence, but rather we have those because we have acted rightly. We are what we repeatedly do. Excellence, then, is not an act but a habit.

—Aristotle

CASE STUDY

She cleaned the kitchen counter with half-hearted gestures. Her hand moved over the peanut butter and jelly concoction. The mess oozed out from the sandwich she had been preparing for her 2-year old son. Thoughts ran rapidly through her mind—like the tap water running through the sponge filled with gooey mess.

Her thoughts wandered to a different time and place where she was free to go and do as she pleased.

This was not what she had anticipated for marriage. Three children under the age of 8 … a husband gone more often than he was at home, and a house that overwhelmed her more than gave her joy … thoughts of displeasure crept into her mind, thoughts as unattractive as the smeared jelly on the counter.

She wondered what life would be like if she was not tied to the mundane routine of marriage. Her thoughts wandered to a different time and place where she was free to go and do as she pleased … when different men pursued her and life was more romantic and exciting.

It was time to watch her afternoon soap operas. She liked this daily escape from her routine. After a couple of hours she found herself dwelling on negative things again. She would wander into "what if's." What if she had married the other man she had known during her dating years? Or, what if she had pursued a career instead of being a victim of boring and humdrum days? What if she was married to someone who was more romantic and sensitive? Her mind gave way to thoughts of single life and working with those who appreciated her insights and abilities again. After all, she felt that her time at work was exciting and glamorous compared to the messes she regularly found at home.

As women, we can sometimes feel inadequate in what we do as wives and mothers. In our minds we can play "what if" and find refuge in fantasizing about a better time or place. Even though our desire is to have a satisfied husband, behaving children, and a comfortable home, we sometimes find ourselves thinking negative and often destructive thoughts. Thinking about what is excellent goes much deeper than determining to keep a meticulous home, pursuing a promising career, or being a great children's taxi-driver. Thinking about what is excellent requires that a woman focus her mind on God's direction for her life.

BASIC TRAINING

Personal Time

(30-45 Minutes)

Answer the following questions individually before your group meeting.

1. What were some of the things the woman in the case study struggled with in her thoughts? How did allowing her thoughts to dwell on "what if's" create a negative environment?

2. How do you think her daily dose of afternoon soap operas affected her thoughts?

3. In what ways can you relate to her struggles?

Thinking about what is excellent requires that a woman focus her mind on God's direction for her life.

4. What other issues do you think a typical woman struggles with in her thought life? In what ways are these contrary to God's desire for her?

In Philippians 4:8, we are told to let our minds dwell on what is "excellent." Pursuing excellence, according to the world, is doing well in a job or position. However, there is more to *being* excellent than merely acting a certain way. God calls us to pursue moral excellence. Moral excellence is achieved by making right choices in what we allow ourselves to watch—by not looking at pornography or inappropriate movies. Moral excellence is also developed by choosing where we go and who we spend time with, either individually or as a couple. All of these choices are made with God's help and guidance.

5. How does the world measure excellence? Do you think the world views moral excellence as important? Why?

6. How would you help the woman in the case study understand the importance of excellence in thinking about her marriage?

7. How does what we watch and read affect the pursuit of moral excellence?

8. We guide our children in what they watch, yet sometimes allow ourselves to do what we don't want them to do. Can you think of some examples of this?

Moral excellence is God's desire for each of us. He wants us to makes choices not merely because it will enhance our personal development, or because it will give us greater credibility with others, but because God knows that what we choose to pursue will ultimately affect who we become—women of excellence.

ADVANCED TRAINING

Group Interaction Time
(60 Minutes)

Discuss the following in your group.

Paul's challenge to the Philippians was to be Christ-minded. As we've learned in this study, becoming Christ-minded includes dwelling on what is true, honorable, right, pure, lovely, of good repute. In this chapter we look at the next item on Paul's list: excellence.

Paul's challenge to the Philippians was to be Christ-minded.

Paul recognized that if those in Philippi did not grasp the importance of dwelling on excellence according to God's perspective, they would become consumed by the enticements of the world. They would try to achieve excellence using the world's standards—by looking good externally. But Paul wanted his readers to be morally excellent— *internally*—according to God's standards.

1. Share with the group some of the things from your personal time about how women struggle in their thought life. Share how the woman in the case study struggled in her thought life.

Paul's earthly goal was to pursue God with moral excellence until His race was complete.

2. Why do you think God wants us to pursue moral excellence not only in our actions but also in our thought life? Why would moral excellence be necessary in a relationship between a husband and wife?

3. What typical issues do couples face regarding moral excellence in marriage?

Paul never described himself as an athlete in the physical sense. Instead, he referred to himself as a spiritual athlete, and he illustrated progress in the Christian life by describing a runner.

> *Do you not know that those who run in a race all run, but only one receives the prize? Run in such a way that you may win. And everyone who competes in the games exercises self-control in all things. They then do it to receive a perishable wreath, but we an imperishable. Therefore I run in such a way, as not without aim; I box in such a way as not beating the air; but I buffet my body and make it my slave, lest possibly, after I have preached to others, I myself should be disqualified.*
>
> —1 Corinthians 9:24-27

He knew that he and other believers would not be perfected until the day of Christ. Paul's earthly goal was to pursue God with moral excellence until His race was complete. His desire was to run his spiritual race with perseverance.

> *I press on toward the goal for the prize of the upward call of God in Christ Jesus.*
>
> —Philippians 3:14

First Standard: Pursuing Christ's Example of Moral Excellence

4. Read Hebrews 12:1-3:

> *Therefore, since we have so great a cloud of witnesses surrounding us, let us also lay aside every encumbrance, and the sin which so easily entangles us, and let us run with endurance the race that is set before us, fixing our eyes on Jesus, the author and perfecter of faith, who for the joy set before Him endured the cross, despising the shame, and has sat down at the right hand of the throne of God. For consider Him who has endured such hostility by sinners against Himself, so that you may not grow weary and lose heart.*

... let us run with endurance the race that is set before us, fixing our eyes on Jesus ...

What would be some examples of encumbrances or sins that keep us from running "the race that is set before us?"

5. What sins might entangle us when running a morally excellent race in marriage?

6. How can we, as followers of Christ, fix our eyes on Jesus while running the race?

We are called to gird our minds for action. Girding means to restrain, tighten, bring under control.

7. Galatians 6:9 urges us to "not lose heart in doing good, for in due time we shall reap if we do not grow weary."

When have you been tempted to "lose heart in doing good?" How can keeping our eyes on Christ help us to not grow weary?

Second Standard: Pursuing Moral Excellence in Our Thoughts

Therefore, gird your minds for action, keep sober in spirit, fix your hope completely on the grace to be brought to you at the revelation of Jesus Christ.

—Peter 1:13

We are called to gird our minds for action. Girding means to restrain, tighten, bring under control. In a race we bring physical skills under control with self-discipline and determination. We must also bring our minds under control in the same way.

8. What ways can we discipline our minds like a runner disciplines himself for a race?

9. Disciplining our minds involves choosing what we allow our thoughts to dwell on. What type of things are we often tempted to dwell upon that *do not* encourage moral excellence?

10. What can we dwell upon that *does* encourage moral excellence?

11. Write out three things you can change which will have an impact in your thought life (i.e. books you read, TV you watch, etc). Share one of your ideas with the group.

Third Standard: Pursuing Excellent Thinking in Our Homes

Once we recognize Christ's example and set our thoughts on what is excellent, it's time to bring our thoughts back to home. Regardless, if you work inside or outside the home, the most challenging place to direct our thoughts to "whatever is excellent" can sometimes be the place we live.

12. How can pursuing "whatever is excellent" in your thoughts create a positive attitude in your heart toward your husband, marriage, and children?

13. What example do you set for your children when you demonstrate an attitude of excellence? Why is this important in their training?

In our marriages and homes, as mothers of our children or workers outside the home, we are called to demonstrate our very best, regardless of the difficulties and challenges. Not "excellence" in the sense that our homes will never be messy or families will never experience disagreements. Not "excellence" where no mistakes are made or trials never occur. Instead, we are called to a greater sense of excellence that surpasses what the world views as achievement and perfection, beauty and popularity.

Our goal as women and wives should be toward the excellence God desires for our lives. His excellence is shaped in us by the moral choices and decisions, thoughts and actions we take that shape us into the women He has designed us to be.

MARCHING ORDERS

(10 minutes)

Take Home Project

1. Now that you know how excellence can be compared to a race, take the time this week to go for a walk. This can be a short, meditative stroll or intense walk-a-thon, but use the time to think about what you have learned this week. Pray and ask God to begin redirecting your thoughts from the negative to the excellent. Just like training for a race, training our minds takes time and determination.

2. Make a date with your husband to cover the husband/wife questions. Pray before your time together. Remember, "Excellent speech is not fitting for a fool" (Proverbs 17:7). Display wisdom instead of folly as you speak.

3. Memorize 1 Peter 1:13: "Therefore, gird your minds for action, keep sober in spirit, fix your hope completely on the grace to be brought to you at the revelation of Jesus Christ. Test each other on this memory verse the next time the group meets.

ON THE HOME FRONT

(20 Minutes)

Discuss/answer the following with your husband.

- Sometimes expressing what you are learning in this study can be difficult. There are times when your husband may need to read the opening story to help him understand what the chapter is all about. It may be useful for him to read the case study. If he doesn't struggle with your particular issues, you may instead want to take the time to share with him what you learned from the study: How we are called to run a race of excellence by using Christ as our example, setting our thoughts on what is excellent, and pursuing excellence in our homes, beginning with our thought life.

- Can dwelling on what is excellent change a person's heart and attitude?

- How could this affect a marriage?

- What specific things are excellent about our marriage?

- Can we agree to dwell on one area of excellence in our marriage this week and then share next week how this has changed our attitudes?

Notes

CHAPTER NINE:
If Anything is Worthy of Praise

CASE STUDY

The door closed quietly. He entered the house as if for the first time, and wondered how long it would take to feel like this was his home again. Each time he left and came back from a deployment or TDY he experienced the same feelings. The only problem was he could never quite pinpoint those feelings or describe them to his wife. He knew she recognized the difference in him and she was always agreeable to give him some time and space. But how long could he expect her to wait on him … especially since he couldn't verbalize what was going on?

Each time they knew they would once again be apart they slid into a honeymoon mentality.

The cycle of their relationship was predictable—if predictable was really the right word. Their attitudes toward each other before, during, and after each separation were as unpredictable as the weather. What *did* seem predictable was the cycle of saying goodbye and reuniting. Each time they knew they would once again be apart they slid into a honeymoon mentality. She showered him with love and admiration. He seemed more willing to overlook some of the small things that annoyed him about her. He expressed his undying love and praise to her more than normal and truly meant every word.

Then the cycle of leaving began. Paperwork, packing, and other preparations all took precedence over their loving accolades toward each other. Short tempers, frustrations, and fears replaced holding hands, kissing, and intimacy. By the time he left, they would still demonstrate love but he knew the strain on their relationship had taken its toll.
Once apart, they would slide into their separate lives. She took care of bills, babies, and being a long-distance lover to him. He would become consumed with life away from home, not allowing himself to dwell on the family he loved.

Now he was home once again. What he needed more than anything from his wife was words of support telling him they would get through this time together. He wished he could tell her how important her words of encouragement were to him—how important their relationship was to him—especially when he first arrived home. What words could he use to express his need for her love and respect? When all was said and done, what he wanted most was the predictability of her praise each and every time he returned. The question always remained … would he receive it?

BASIC TRAINING

Personal Time

(30-45 Minutes)

Answer the following questions individually before your group meeting.

1. Describe the cycle the case study couple experienced when they had a deployment.

2. Why do you think the husband described in the case study needed to hear approval from his wife, especially on his return?

3. Proverbs 12:18 says, "There is one who speaks rashly like the thrusts of a sword, but the tongue of the wise brings healing." What have you found to be effective ways to praise your husband before, during, and after a deployment?

"There is one who speaks rashly like the thrusts of a sword, but the tongue of the wise brings healing."

4. In what other situations does your husband need words of praise and encouragement from you?

5. How does he respond when you praise him? How does he respond to criticism?

ADVANCED TRAINING

Group Interaction Time
(60 Minutes)

Discuss the following in your group.

Paul praised Christ because he knew he was a forgiven man, and therefore Christ was worthy of his praise.

In this study we have looked at Paul's challenge in Philippians 4:8 to "let your mind dwell on these things." The "things" Paul speaks of are:

- Whatever is true
- Whatever is honorable
- Whatever is right
- Whatever is pure
- Whatever is lovely
- Whatever is of good repute
- If there is any excellence

In this chapter we come to the final item on Paul's list. He calls us to dwell on "anything worthy of praise." For Christians, this first calls to mind our need to praise God.

The apostle Paul praised Christ at every opportunity. He sang praises in prison and praised Him while being persecuted. Paul praised Christ because he knew he was a forgiven man, and therefore Christ was worthy of his praise. For this reason Paul could write about rejoicing and being content in all circumstances. His positive responses during the difficult times in his life were due to his ability to praise God.

Paul demonstrated this during his first visit to Philippi, when the church there was established:

> *… we ran a straight course to Samothrace, and on the day following to Neapolis, and from there to Philippi, which is a leading city of the district of Macedonia, a Roman colony; and we were staying in this city for some days. And a certain woman named Lydia, a seller of purple fabrics, a worshiper of God, was listening; and the Lord opened her heart to respond to the things spoken by Paul.*
>
> —Acts 16:11b-12,14

During Paul's stay in Philippi, however, he and his companions were seized, beaten, and put into prison.

> *And when they had inflicted many blows upon them, they threw them into prison, commanding the jailer to guard them securely.*
>
> —Acts 16:23

What was Paul's response?

> *But about midnight Paul and Silas (in prison) were praying and singing hymns of praise to God, and the prisoners were listening to them.*
>
> —Acts 16:25

Paul praised God no matter where he found himself or how difficult the circumstances. Scripture is very specific in telling us who deserves all praise.

Praising God in Every Circumstance

1. Read Psalm 145:1-7:

> *I will extol Thee, my God, O King; and I will bless Thy name forever and ever. Every day I will bless Thee, and I will praise Thy name forever and ever. Great is the Lord, and highly to be praised; and His greatness is unsearchable. One generation shall praise Thy works to another, and shall declare Thy mighty acts. On the glorious splendor of Thy majesty, and on Thy wonderful works, I will meditate. And men shall speak of the power of Thine awesome acts; and I will tell of Thy greatness. They shall eagerly utter the memory of Thine abundant goodness, and shall shout joyfully of Thy righteousness.*

One generation shall praise Thy works to another, and shall declare Thy mighty acts.

Verse five reads " … on Thy wonderful works, I will meditate." What are some "wonderful works" that God has done in your life? Take a couple of minutes to write a short list and then share it with the group.

... we also are told to take great care in the words we speak.

2. Now read Psalm 145:14-18:

The Lord sustains all who fall, and raises up all who are bowed down. The eyes of all look to Thee, and Thou dost give them their food in due time. Thou dost open Thy hand, and dost satisfy the desire of every living thing. The Lord is righteous in all His ways, and kind in all His deeds. The Lord is near to all who call upon Him, to all who call upon Him in truth.

Just like Paul, we are called to seek God and praise Him in whatever circumstance we find ourselves. Why do you think it's sometimes difficult to praise God when we are suffering or going through severe trials?

3. Psalm 145:14 says "The Lord sustains all who fall, and raises up all who are bowed down." What is an example of a time when God sustained you during a difficult circumstance?

4. How is our attitude affected when we spend time focusing on what God has done for us?

The Power of Our Words

Not only are we commanded to praise God, but we also are told to take great care in the words we speak. The Bible speaks of the power of the "tongue" in numerous passages. For example:

> *... the tongue is a small part of the body, and yet it boasts of great things. Behold how great a forest is set aflame by such a small fire! And the tongue is a fire, the very world of iniquity; the tongue is set among our members as that which defiles the entire body, and sets on fire the course of our life, and is set on fire by hell. For every species of beasts and birds, of reptiles and creatures of the sea, is tamed, and has been tamed by the human race. But no one can tame the tongue; it is a restless evil and full of deadly poison. With it we bless our Lord and Father; and with it we curse men, who have been made in the likeness of God; from the same mouth come both blessing and cursing ...*
>
> —James 3:5-10a

... no one can tame the tongue; it is a restless evil and full of deadly poison. With it we bless our Lord and Father; and with it we curse men, who have been made in the likeness of God ...

5. In what ways can our words be like a forest fire? Like poison?

6. Read the following passages:

A soothing tongue is a tree of life, but perversion in it crushes the spirit.

—Proverbs 15:4

There is one who speaks rashly like the thrusts of a sword, but the tongue of the wise brings healing.

—Proverbs 12:18

A man has joy in an apt answer, and how delightful is a timely word.

—Proverbs 15:23

7. Tell about a time from your childhood when someone criticized you, and a time when someone praised you. How did those words affect you?

8. Why do you remember those words after all these years?

9. How can your words be a "tree of life" to your husband? Can you think of one time when you saw the positive results of this in your marriage relationship?

Praising Our Husbands

As wives, we sometimes find it easier to praise our children, our parents, or our friends. But when it comes to praising our husbands we may find that words do not come easily.

10. Share your answers to these questions from your personal time:
In what types of situations does your husband need words of praise and encouragement?

How does he respond when you praise him? How does he respond to criticism?

11. Why do people need to be praised for what they do right? How does this affect a person's self-worth?

12. Share two things your husband does well.

13. As a group, decide on several ways to support your husbands with praise while they are deployed. How can having a "praise plan" in place before your husband leaves prepare you for your time apart?

MARCHING ORDERS

(10 minutes)

Take Home Project

1. Honestly assess how you talk to your husband when he comes home from work. Are you critical or do you give encouragement when needed? Develop one point of action of how you can change critical words into encouraging ones. Ask someone in the group to keep you accountable.

2. There are two ways to use the one tongue that God has given you—either to praise or to harm. Next time you are in the company of your spouse think twice about what you say. Remember, we have two ears and one mouth so try to keep quiet twice as long as you allow your tongue to speak.

Take a few minutes to memorize Psalm 34:13: "Keep your tongue from evil, and your lips from speaking deceit."

3. Make a date with your husband to review the husband/wife questions. Pray before you meet, asking God to guard your tongue from speaking harm to him. Remember that our tongue is either a fiery dart or a healing balm.

4. Write your husband a letter telling him why you are proud of who he is, who God wants him to become, and what he does for your family. It can be either short or long, just make sure that it is filled with praise!

ON THE HOME FRONT

(20 Minutes)

Discuss the following with your husband.

Time apart due to deployments or job-related separations can take its toll on a relationship. Sometimes the unpredictability of military life forces a couple to focus on preparations for leaving and returning home so they don't have to face loneliness or fears of being apart. The problem with concentrating only on the external realities of what needs to be done can cause a couple to not meet each other's needs of praise, approval, and love.

Sometimes the unpredictability of military life forces a couple to focus on preparations for leaving and returning home so they don't have to face loneliness or fears of being apart.

This week the focus was on praise. In order to praise one another we must first praise God in the midst of our circumstances. We must then realize the significance of words and the awesome power we have with our tongue. As a couple, it is important to take time to praise each other, whether together or apart.

- Do I give you enough words of praise and/or encouragement?

____

____

____

____

____

- What words of encouragement/praise are especially useful to you?

- Do I often neglect to demonstrate praise when you need it?

- What is one thing we can do to remember to praise each other in the midst of separations?

- What significance do my words of praise have on your life? How can I praise you more effectively?

CHAPTER TEN:
Loving Your Military Man for a Lifetime

It was over—finally finished. The suffering we had seen my father-in-law, Jesse, endure for several days had run its course. He had completed his race with dignity. Watching him suffer had been a tiring ordeal, particularly for Jim's mom, Jane. She had known, loved, and shared nearly 50 years of joy and bittersweet sadness in their marriage. Together they had raised six children.

How many times do we watch an elderly couple hold hands and pray that our own marriages will succeed?

In the 30 years of their military life together, he had fought in three wars—World War II, Korea, and Vietnam. Every time duty required him to leave, Jane held their home intact. She had suffered with him through the loss of their youngest daughter to a rare blood cancer. Now Jane waited and watched as Jesse's once strong body was wracked with pain from the curse of cancer. She kissed his face one last time and said goodbye.

Loving someone is demonstrated not only during the easy times, the happy and enjoyable times. The vows spoken before God in the presence of witnesses calls for a love "until death do us part." Loving includes the difficult days, the days spent apart, the days weeping together over hurts and losses. Loving for a lifetime includes it all—birth, life, and death. It includes caring, laughing, and crying while rearing and releasing children. Watching Jane say goodbye to her hero, her military man, brought sadness and grief, but it demonstrated a lovely thing—an exquisite thing—the love of a lifetime.

> *Day is done, gone the sun; from the lake, from the hills, from the sky. Safely rest, all is well. God is nigh.*
>
> —From the military bugle call "Taps"

BASIC TRAINING

Personal Time
(30-45 Minutes)

Answer the following questions individually before your group meeting.

How many times do we watch an elderly couple hold hands and pray that our own marriages will succeed? We are not as enamored when we see young couples embrace because we know they haven't tested the waters of loving someone for better or worse, in sickness and in health. We know they haven't yet worked through the best of times and the worst of times. However, when we see a mature couple still in love we understand they have worked at their relationship and have learned to love over a lifetime.

1. What do you think loving for a lifetime includes?

2. What have you seen in couples who have been married for a significant number of years that you want to emulate in your own marriage? Why are these things significant to you?

3. When you have been married 50 years, what would you like others to say about your marriage?

This study was written in order to help military wives realize their marriages are unique. They are unique in the sense that couples in the military are constantly aware of the world's political situation and its impact on their family. They are unique because they encounter lengthy separations and raise children who long to see a parent who has spent many months or years away from home.

Yet, like their civilian counterparts, they want their marriages to succeed. They long to be an example to other couples of how a marriage can endure the difficult, the challenging, and yet survive.

4. What would you like your children to take into their marriages that you have demonstrated in yours?

5. What have you learned from this study that has helped you recognize the uniqueness of your military marriage?

... couples in the military are constantly aware of the world's political situation and the impact that has on their family.

BASIC TRAINING

Personal Time

(30-45 Minutes)

Answer the following questions individually before your group meeting.

Paul has taught us many things in this study. He has described what it means to rejoice, to trust God, to let your mind dwell on the right things, and to put into practice the things you learn. We have read how Paul taught the Philippians to dwell on what is true, honorable, right, pure, lovely, of good repute, excellent, and praiseworthy. If Paul were with us today he would say that only Christ exemplifies each quality with perfection. Christ was his example, and Christ is ours.

If Paul were with us today he would say that only Christ exemplifies each quality with perfection. Christ was his example, and Christ is ours.

1. Share the one thing you learned from this study that has had a profound effect on you. How has this had an impact on your marriage?

____

____

____

____

2. What would you say has been the biggest challenge from this study to implement in your marriage? Why do you think this has been difficult for you?

____

____

____

____

This study is nearing an end. My desire for *Loving Your Military Man* was to help wives refocus their hearts and minds toward loving their husbands, but more importantly to a lifetime of loving God. Only when I realized God needed to be first in my life was I able to let my marriage be all He intended. Marriage is difficult at times, but a blessing so much more of the time. As women, we need to understand that loving a military man doesn't mean loving him only when times are good, or only when he is good or when I feel good. God calls us to love our man for a lifetime!

3. Share from your personal time:

What do you admire in long-term marriages?

What would you like others to say about your marriage in the future?

What legacy would you like to leave your children through the example of your marriage?

4. List some things you think are absolutely necessary in order for a marriage to last a lifetime.

5. In what situations in a military marriage would you say that sacrificial love is needed most?

6. Have there been times when loving your husband has been an act of will and not a desire in your heart? Give an example.

7. If you had the opportunity to share with a young woman who is about to marry someone on active duty, what would you tell her about loving him in the midst of his career?

8. Choose one thing from the study you would like to apply in your life in the next month. Share what you would like to do so you can pray for each other in the weeks ahead.

Christ is our example and He should be the focus of our thinking. Everything else dwindles with insignificance when we realize we need to fill our thoughts with His Words and our lives with His love. As we dwell on Him, we begin to recognize He forever dwells in us. Christ is the fulfillment of all we are to pursue. He alone is our example. Dwelling on Him and His Word will bring us to a fruitful thought life.

9. In review, why is letting our minds dwell on those things which are true, honorable, right, pure, lovely, of good repute, excellent, and praiseworthy so important in our marriages?

10. What can you do *daily* in order to allow God to help you keep your mind on those things cited by Paul?

My prayer as you finish this study is that you will commit your marriage to the marriage maker—Jesus. I also pray that, as a military wife, you will view your life as an adventure filled with excitement and joy. But most of all, I pray that you will be willing to climb out on a limb for your husband by *Loving Your Military Man*.

MARCHING ORDERS

(10 minutes)

Take Home Project

1. Now that you have completed this study, what will your response be? Have you prayed and received Jesus into your heart (See Appendix A)? Have you understood what it means to dwell on "the best?" If you have said "no" to any of these questions, then stop right now and ask God to open your heart to the changes you need to make in order to love your husband with an everlasting love.

2. Make a date with your husband to go over the husband/wife questions. Pray about your time together before you meet. Forget what has happened in the past, dwell on the good, and begin to realize Jesus is the One who meets all of your needs. Remember, your husband may disappoint you at times, but you are not living in a fairy tale and you don't want to end up in a failure tale.

3. Be sure to keep Philippians 4:8 in your mind at all times: … *Finally, brethren, whatever is true, whatever is honorable, whatever is right, whatever is pure, whatever is lovely, whatever is of good repute, if there is any excellence, and if anything worthy of praise, let your mind dwell on these things.*

4. If you know other women who would benefit from learning how to love their husbands, make a commitment to take them through this or a similar study.

ON THE HOME FRONT

(20 Minutes)

Discuss/answer the following with your husband.

Once you have answered the questions below you can tell your husband his commitment to answer questions for this study is finished. Perhaps this type of interaction has been less threatening to him than attending other types of studies. Thank him for participating in the study and making your experience more complete because he has been a part of your learning.

- What would you say is the best thing about our marriage?

- What would we want for others to say about our love for each other after we have been married for a lifetime? What can we start doing now to achieve this?

- How have I effectively shown you my love?

- What one thing can I change that would better demonstrate my love to you?

- Have you seen any change in me as a result of this study?

____

____

____

- **If your husband feels comfortable doing this, ask him to pray for you and your marriage.** Ask Jesus to give you love for each other—a beautiful love that will be a picture to others of how marriage was intended to be.

- Commit your marriage to the Marriage Maker. Then sign the statement below together:

  In our marriage, I am committed to dwelling on those things that are true, honorable, right, pure, lovely, of good repute, excellent, and praiseworthy. And, I am committed to put into practice those things God has taught me through this study about marriage and loving my spouse.

  ____

  Signature/date

  ____

  Signature/date

Where Do You Go From Here?

It is my prayer that you have benefited greatly from this study and are now closer to God and your husband. May you continue to grow in your love toward God and your military man as you build your relationship according to His Word.

If you have enjoyed meeting with other women as you worked through this study, you may want to consider leading a group of women who are unfamiliar with Scripture, or who would like to grow in their spiritual walk. Perhaps you may want to continue meeting with the same women using many of the available women's studies.

Or, you and your husband may want to participate in a HomeBuilders Couples Series® or a HomeBuilders Parenting Series® study, possibly with other couples from your women's group. A great first study would be *Defending the Military Marriage*, which addresses numerous challenges you face as a military couple. There are now many studies in the HomeBuilders Couples Series and HomeBuilders Parenting Series that cover a variety of topics.

I would also encourage you to attend a FamilyLife Weekend to Remember® conference or a Military Marriage seminar. These weekend conferences will provide an intensive and encouraging opportunity to strengthen your marriage.

For more information, contact:

Military Ministry Seminars
Military Ministry
PO Box 120124
Newport News, VA 23612
1-800-444-6006

Weekend to Remember
FamilyLife
5800 Ranch Drive
Little Rock, AR 72223
1-800-FL-TODAY

I hope you will begin reaching out to strengthen other women and marriages in your community and in your chapel or church.

—Bea Fishback, author

"Praying While Apart" Prayer Calendar

	Sunday	Monday	Tuesday	Wednesday	Thursday	Friday	Saturday
Pre-deployment	**Theme:** The Lord is our strength and our shield; our hearts trust in Him **Scripture:** Psalm 28	**Theme:** We shall seek God earnestly **Scripture:** Psalm 63	**Theme:** Trusting in our heavenly Father **Scripture:** Psalm 37	**Theme:** Seeking God's mercy **Scripture:** Psalm 51	**Theme:** God's unfailing love **Scripture:** Psalm 33	**Theme:** Seeking God wholeheartedly **Scripture:** Jeremiah 29:13	**Theme:** Finding success by following God's commands **Scripture:** Joshua 1:7-9
Deployment	**Theme:** Trusting in God with all our heart **Scripture:** Proverbs 3	**Theme:** Deliverance from fears **Scripture:** Psalm 34	**Theme:** Seeking refuge in God **Scripture:** Psalm 91	**Theme:** Fellowship with the Father and the Son, Jesus **Scripture:** 1 John 1:3	**Theme:** Seeking God **Scripture:** Psalm 77	**Theme:** Praying to a God who listens to our needs **Scripture:** Nehemiah 1:11	**Theme:** The God who knows us and knows our needs **Scripture:** Psalm 139
Reunion	**Theme:** Thanking God **Scripture:** Psalm 77	**Theme:** God's goodness **Scripture:** Psalm 100	**Theme:** God's love and faithfulness **Scripture:** Psalm 138	**Theme:** God's plans for us **Scripture:** Jeremiah 29:11	**Theme:** The joy of reuniting with your spouse **Scripture:** Song of Solomon 2:16	**Theme:** Showing love for others **Scripture:** 1 Corinthians 13	**Theme:** Praying and giving thanks continually **Scripture:** 1 Thessalonians. 5:16
The Armor of God	**Theme:** Be strong in the Lord **Scripture:** Ephesians 6: 10-18	**Theme:** Belt of Truth **Scripture:** Philippians 4:8	**Theme:** Shield of Faith **Scripture:** Hebrews 11:1	**Theme:** Breastplate of Righteousness **Scripture:** Philippians 1:9	**Theme:** The Gospel of Peace **Scripture:** Ephesians 4:1-3	**Theme:** Helmet of Salvation **Scripture:** John 3:16	**Theme:** Sword of the Spirit **Scripture:** Philippians 1:9
Your Family Prayer Requests							

*Contributed by Carleene Myer

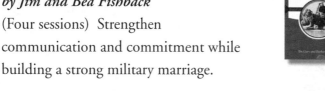

The HomeBuilders Couples Series®

Defending the Military Marriage

by Jim and Bea Fishback

(Four sessions) Strengthen communication and commitment while building a strong military marriage.

Keeping Your Covenant

by various authors

(Four sessions) Get an introductory overview and examine lessons from four different HomeBuilders series.

Building Your Marriage

by Dennis Rainey

(Seven sessions) Learn about and apply God's basic blueprint for a strong, healthy marriage.

Building Teamwork in Your Marriage

by Robert Lewis and Dave Boehi

(Six sessions) Discover how you are uniquely equipped and that differences are a gift from God.

Building Your Mate's Self-Esteem

by Dennis and Barbara Rainey

(Seven sessions) Improve marriage by encouraging and discovering new levels of love and fulfillment.

Growing Together in Christ

by David Sunde

(Six sessions) Unleash power and joy as you and your spouse develop a daily relationship with Christ.

Improving Communication in Your Marriage

by Gary and Barbara Rosberg

(Six sessions) Enhance communication skills and resolve conflict scripturally.

Making Your Remarriage Last

by Jim Keller

(Six sessions) Recognize and address the unique challenges remarried couples face in building a godly marriage.

Mastering Money in Your Marriage

by Ron Blue

(Six sessions) Learn to manage money wisely. Discover how money issues can be a tool for growth and not a root of contention.

Overcoming Stress in Your Marriage

by Doug Daily

(Six sessions) Make life less hectic and more meaningful as family priorities are established based on biblical principles.

Resolving Conflict in Your Marriage

by Bob and Jan Horner

(Six sessions) Transform conflicts into growth opportunities and grow in love for your spouse.

First Responder Marriage

by Chuck Douglas

(Four sessions) Address the diverse issues facing "first responder" marriages and learn to handle the extraordinary relationship stress.

HomeBuilders Leader Guide

By Drew and Kit Coons

Host groups effectively with tips for starting a HomeBuilders study.

The HomeBuilders Parenting Series®

Defending the Military Family

by Jim and Bea Fishback

(Five sessions) Gain a better understanding of the unique parenting challenges of military families.

Building Character in Your Children

By Crawford and Karen Loritts

(Six sessions) Discover ways to build life changing character qualities that deepen understanding and enhance communication.

Establishing Effective Discipline for Your Children

By Dennis and Barbara Rainey

(Six sessions) Gain insight on the importance and connection between rules and relationships.

Helping Your Children Know God

By Bob Lepine

(Six sessions) Equip children to set standards and develop convictions for knowing and relating to God.

Guiding Your Teenagers

By Dennis and Barbara Rainey

(Six sessions) Help your teen make positive memories while resisting unhealthy peer pressure and adolescent traps.

Improving Your Parenting

By Dennis and Barbara Rainey

(Six sessions) Strengthen the spiritual foundation in your home by examining Scripture, sharing, and praying together.

Raising Children of Faith

By Dennis and Barbara Rainey

(Six sessions) Lead children into a relationship with God filled with an understanding of His purpose for them.

Considering Adoption

by Doug and Amy Martin, and Jason and Tricia Weber

(Five sessions) Address your questions and concerns to decide whether adoption is the right choice for you.

Visit Military Ministry Online ...

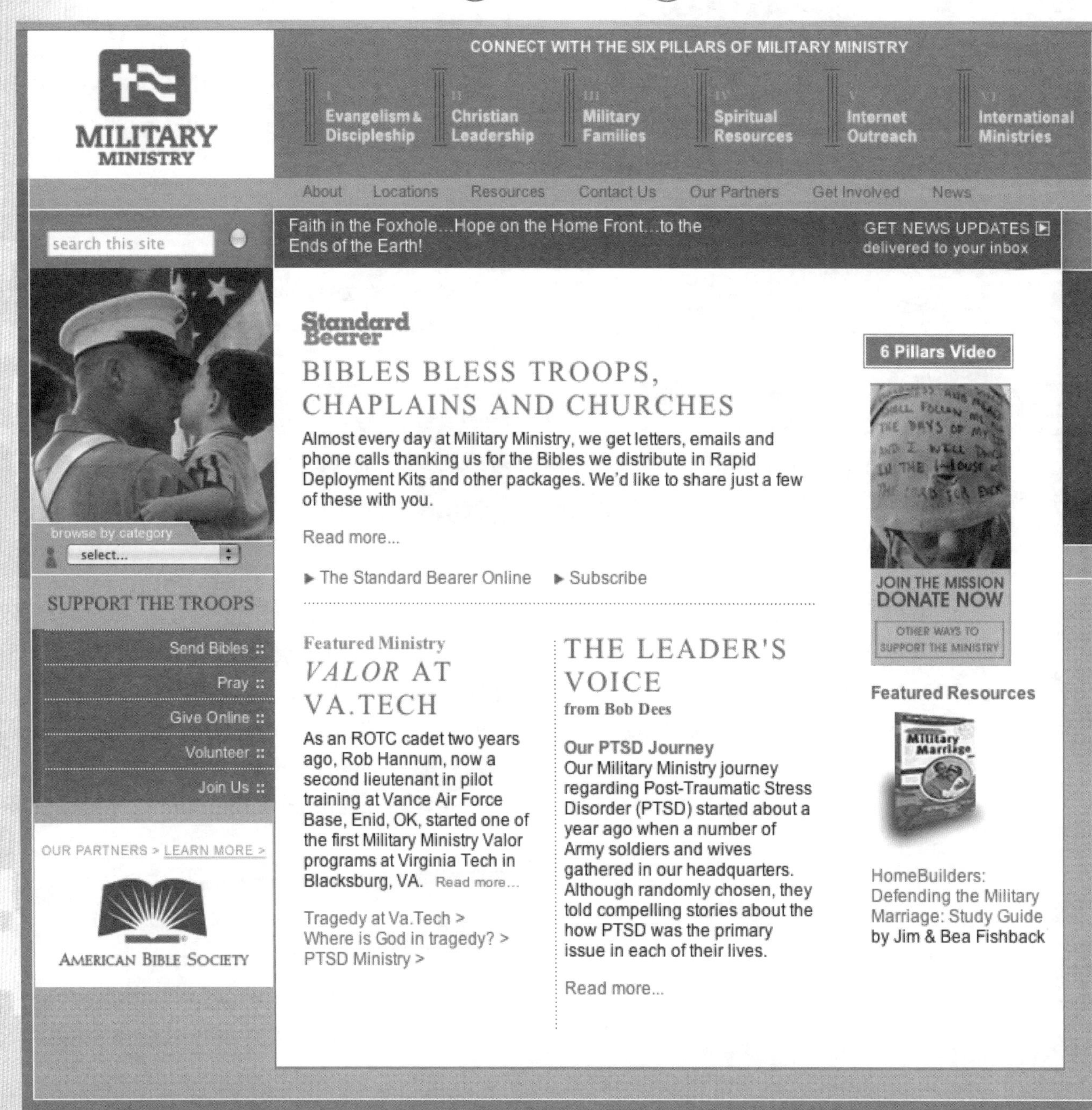

MILITARY MINISTRY
CONNECT WITH THE SIX PILLARS OF MILITARY MINISTRY
Evangelism & Discipleship
Christian Leadership
Military Families
Spiritual Resources
Internet Outreach
International Ministries
About Locations Resources Contact Us Our Partners Get Involved News
search this site
Faith in the Foxhole...Hope on the Home Front...to the Ends of the Earth!
GET NEWS UPDATES delivered to your inbox
browse by category
select...
SUPPORT THE TROOPS
Send Bibles ::
Pray ::
Give Online ::
Volunteer ::
Join Us ::
OUR PARTNERS > LEARN MORE >
AMERICAN BIBLE SOCIETY
Standard Bearer
BIBLES BLESS TROOPS, CHAPLAINS AND CHURCHES
Almost every day at Military Ministry, we get letters, emails and phone calls thanking us for the Bibles we distribute in Rapid Deployment Kits and other packages. We'd like to share just a few of these with you.
Read more...
The Standard Bearer Online
Subscribe
Featured Ministry
VALOR AT VA.TECH
As an ROTC cadet two years ago, Rob Hannum, now a second lieutenant in pilot training at Vance Air Force Base, Enid, OK, started one of the first Military Ministry Valor programs at Virginia Tech in Blacksburg, VA. Read more...
Tragedy at Va.Tech >
Where is God in tragedy? >
PTSD Ministry >
THE LEADER'S VOICE
from Bob Dees
Our PTSD Journey
Our Military Ministry journey regarding Post-Traumatic Stress Disorder (PTSD) started about a year ago when a number of Army soldiers and wives gathered in our headquarters. Although randomly chosen, they told compelling stories about the how PTSD was the primary issue in each of their lives.
Read more...
6 Pillars Video
JOIN THE MISSION
DONATE NOW
OTHER WAYS TO SUPPORT THE MINISTRY
Featured Resources
Military Marriage
HomeBuilders: Defending the Military Marriage: Study Guide by Jim & Bea Fishback
Copyright 2007 The Military Ministry
6060 Jefferson Avenue, Suite 6012, Newport News, VA 23605, 1-800-444-6006
A division of Campus Crusade for Christ International
Contact Us / Send Feedback | Privacy Policy
RSS Feed
solutions by: SILAS PARTNERS

WWW.MILMIN.ORG

APPENDIX A
Experiencing God's Power

Introduction

- For those who seek it, God provides the necessary power to fulfill His purposes and to carry out His plan for oneness.

- We experience this power by knowing God, and by allowing His Spirit to control our lives by faith.

1. God loves you and created you for a relationship with Him.

a. God loves you.

For God so loved the world, that He gave His only begotten Son, that whoever believes in Him shall not perish, but have eternal life.

—John 3:16

b. God wants you to know Him.

And this is eternal life, that they may know You, the only true God, and Jesus Christ whom You have sent.

—John 17:3

What prevents us from knowing God personally?

2. Humanity is separated from God and cannot know Him personally or experience His love and power.

a. All of us are sinful.

For all have sinned and fall short of the glory of God.

—Romans 3:23

b. Our sin separates us from God.

For the wages of sin is death …

—Romans 6:23a

How can the gulf between God and man be bridged?

3. Jesus Christ is God's only provision for our sin. Through Him alone we can know God personally and experience His love.

a. God became a man in the Person of Jesus Christ.

The Word [Jesus] became flesh, and dwelt among us, and we saw His glory, glory as of the only begotten from the Father, full of grace and truth.

—John 1:14

b. He died in our place.

But God demonstrates His own love toward us, in that while we were yet sinners, Christ died for us.

—Romans 5:8

c. He rose from the dead.

Christ died for our sins … He was buried … He was raised on the third day according to the Scriptures … He appeared to Cephas (Peter), then to the twelve. After that He appeared to more than five hundred …

—1 Corinthians 15:3-6

d. He is the only way to God.

Jesus said to him, "I am the way, and the truth, and the life; no one comes to the Father, but through Me."

—John 14:6

4. We must individually receive Jesus Christ as Savior and Lord; then we can know God personally and experience His love.

a. We must change our minds about the way we have lived.

b. We must receive Christ by accepting the free gift of salvation He offers us.

But as many as received Him, to them He gave the right to become children of God, even to those who believe in His name.

—John 1:12

For by grace you have been saved through faith; and that not of yourselves, it is the gift of God; not as a result of works, so that no one may boast.

—Ephesians 2:8-9

Self-Directed Life

Christ-Directed Life

5. What are the results of placing my faith in Jesus Christ?

The Bible says:

a. My sins are forgiven (Colossians 2:13).

b. I possess the gift of eternal life.

And the testimony is this, that God has given us eternal life, and this life is in His Son.

—1 John 5:11

c. I have been given the Holy Spirit to empower me to pursue intimacy with God and oneness with my spouse.

6. I can respond to God right now by faith through prayer.

A suggested life-changing decision: "Lord Jesus, I need You. Thank You for dying on the cross for my sins. I acknowledge that I am a sinner and I am separated from You. Please forgive me. I receive You as my Savior and Lord. Thank You for forgiving my sins and giving me eternal life. Please take control of my life. Make me the kind of person You want me to be."

____

Signature

____

Date

APPENDIX B
A Way of Hope

A Word from FamilyLife

Each year, millions of women are abused in the one place they thought they would be safe ... their homes. We have included an excerpt from Leslie J. Barner's helpful booklet, *A Way of Hope* (available through FamilyLife), with two purposes:

- To give abused women hope that their lives can change, and
- To provide some concrete suggestions for how to move toward recovery.

This excerpt is not a comprehensive study or a complete guide on domestic violence, nor does it provide all the necessary answers and help you will need. Our goal in providing this information is to help you understand what is going on in your relationship, to give you insight into what domestic violence is about, and to offer guidance on how to change and rebuild your life and marriage.

Several sections have been adapted (with permission) from resources developed by people who have experience and expertise in the area of domestic violence. However, quoting from these materials does not mean that we endorse them in their entirety.

For the sake of simplicity, we have chosen to use the word "husband" when we refer to the abuser. We realize that many victims of abuse are single and that a growing number of men are abused by their wives. Please read through the material knowing that you may need to adapt it to your specific circumstances.

You may be reading this because you know someone in an abusive situation and you want to help. The material will give you important information that can help you be a supportive friend during this difficult time in her life. You will gain a better understanding about what is happening to your friend, what domestic violence and battering is all about, and how you can best help her. You may then want to pass this information on to your friend or walk through it with her.

It is our prayer that this excerpt will be a way of hope for you or your friend.

A Way of Hope

Seven Steps Toward Breaking the Cycle of Violence in Your Life

Step One: Recognize the Need for Change
Step Two: Understand That Healthy Relationships Have Boundaries
Step Three: Seek Outside Help and Guidance
Step Four: Determine the Level of Danger and Develop a Safety Plan
Step Five: Move Toward Personal Recovery by Establishing a Strong Relationship with God
Step Six: Encourage Your Husband to Get Help
Step Seven: Move Toward Reconciliation

Step One: Recognize the Need for Change

Sara's Story

The story on the following pages is true, but details have been changed to protect the storyteller.

I was 17 years old and about to enter my senior year of high school. I met Kurt, a terrific guy who thought I was "perfect," and we started dating. I thought I was in love.

Kurt lived a couple of hours away, so it was a long-distance relationship (I'm sure my parents were thankful). We talked on the phone every Wednesday for an hour or so. Some weekends, my parents would allow him to spend the weekend at our house with strict rules in force. I was always very obedient and knew not to step out of line.

My first indication that he had a temper was during a weekly phone conversation. Kurt and his dad had just had a fight and he told me he had put his fist through his bedroom wall. When I told my mom about this her comment was, "If he's hitting walls today he might be hitting you tomorrow." I told her he would never do that because he loved me too much.

We were married three weeks after my high school graduation. My parents were devastated that I was not attending college; it had been their dream and mine for years. I had never had any real confidence in my abilities and practically no self-esteem. So I took the easy way out.

Soon I noticed that my new husband was extremely jealous and protective. He accused me of sleeping with his friends. He would not allow me to visit my family; he seemed to feel threatened when anyone took attention away from him. When my parents would come into town to visit, he wouldn't allow me to go shopping with my mom or spend time with them. He didn't allow me to go anywhere without him and only he could drive our vehicle.

Even worse, I was becoming afraid of him. He had begun to fly into rages for no apparent reason. Up to this point the worst that had happened were horrible arguments and lots of tears. Every outburst was followed by flowers and apologies that he wouldn't do it again.

Then I found out I was pregnant. Kurt seemed so happy and anxious. Then within a few months it seemed that all hell broke loose. It started one day as we were driving. He said this child couldn't be his, that he knew I had been with someone else, then he began screaming and calling me names. Then his fist seemed to come out of nowhere—hitting me in the stomach! I remember grabbing my stomach, doubling over, and moaning out loud. I was terrified that he had hurt the baby and I really couldn't believe what had just happened!

Kurt immediately pulled off the road and tried to hug me as his tears flowed. He kept asking me to forgive him, and he promised it would never happen again. I was hurting so bad I just wanted to die.

He kept his word for a few weeks. But then he flew into a rage one night and began throwing things and breaking anything in his path. This continued off and on until our son was born. Then life truly became a living hell.

The rages were even more frequent; now Kurt was convinced that I was sleeping with my coworkers. Nothing I said could convince him that I wasn't. The physical abuse really began at this point. I tried to cover the bruises with makeup or with long sleeves. I was so afraid my coworkers would find out, I couldn't bear the embarrassment.

Kurt began calling me at work to "check up on me." Then he started missing work and sitting in the adjoining parking lot so he could watch my office building. I felt alone and confused. I wanted to tell my parents but I was afraid they wouldn't understand.

One night we went to the store and were bringing groceries in when something set him off. I was bringing our son in from the car when Kurt attacked me and shoved me down the stairs. I lost my balance and fell backward with Michael in my arms. I was trying to hold onto him with one arm and trying to stop us with the other. Finally, about halfway down, we landed and blood was everywhere. By the grace of God, our son's arm was only scratched, but my leg and knee were gashed.

I told Kurt that I would kill him if he ever laid another hand on me when our son was nearby. Kurt began crying, apologizing, and begging me to forgive him. I was repulsed by what I saw in him and what I saw in myself. I remember crying out to God and asking Him to protect my son and me.

You Are Not Alone

Your story may not sound exactly like the one you just read, but perhaps you can relate in some ways to her experience. When you are abused you feel desperately alone. You may think, "*Why me? Other women don't have this problem. Something must be wrong with me.*" And you may feel so ashamed that this is happening to you that you don't want anyone to know about it. But the truth is that many wives suffer some form of domestic abuse regardless of racial, religious, educational, or economic backgrounds.

According to the American Medical Association, husbands and boyfriends severely assault as many as four million women every year. One in four women will experience some type of spousal abuse during their lifetime.[1] Many of these women feel trapped, anxious, afraid, and helpless. Some feel they are to blame—that if they could just do better at pleasing their husbands they could change their situations. Others don't know what to do or where to go to get help. Most suffer in silence, hiding their situations from family and friends because of their shame and embarrassment. Or perhaps they fear others will not believe them.

No, you are not alone. But there is hope! Many women have taken bold and courageous steps to seek help, to find freedom from abuse, and to begin the journey toward a new life. Some have even seen their abusers find the help they desperately needed to stop their destructive behavior and experience healing and recovery. Some couples, through intervention and a structured recovery process guided by pastors or qualified counselors, have been able to experience healing and reconciliation in their marriages.

Yes, it is true that change does take time, a lot of courage, and a great deal of support, but change *can* happen. And if you are in an abusive situation, change *must* happen.

What Is Abuse?

A crucial first step in this process will be to acknowledge and understand the abuse occurring in your marriage. Abuse means to mistreat or misuse someone. People abuse others to dominate or control, or to prevent others from making free choices.
There are several different forms of abuse:

- ***Emotional or psychological abuse:*** Mistreating and controlling someone through fear, manipulation, and intimidation, and by attacking that person's sense of self-worth. The abuser seeks to make his wife feel afraid, helpless, confused, and worthless. This form of abuse includes name-calling, mocking, belittling, accusing, blaming, yelling, swearing, harassing, isolating from family and friends, abusing authority, withholding emotional support and affection, and betraying trust.

- ***Physical abuse:*** Assaulting, threatening, or restraining a person through force. Men who batter use physical violence to control women—to scare them into doing whatever they want them to do. Physical abuse includes hitting, slapping, punching, beating, grabbing, shoving, biting, kicking, pulling hair, burning, using or threatening the use of weapons, blocking you from leaving a room or the house during an argument, driving recklessly, or intimidating you with threatening gestures.

- ***Sexual abuse:*** Behavior that dominates or controls someone through sexual acts, demands or insults. Sexual abuse includes making you do sexual things when it is against your will, when you are sick, or when it is painful; using force (including rape in or out of marriage), threats, or coercion to obtain sex or perform sexual acts; forcing you to have unprotected sex, or sex with others; treating you like a sex object, and calling you names like "frigid" or "whore."

Facing the Facts ... And Facing Your Fears

Denying the abuse or the impact of abuse may have helped you to cope with the problem until now. However, denial is also the very thing that will hinder you from breaking the cycle of violence in your life, and from experiencing peace and freedom from abuse. The fact that you are reading this is evidence that you are willing to acknowledge the abuse. You've already taken a courageous step.

Facing the fact that you are being abused or battered by your husband, and that his behavior is not normal, can stir up deep emotional feelings—especially fear. You must acknowledge these fears in order to face and deal with the problem. In her book, *Invisible Wounds—A Self-Help Guide for Women in Destructive Relationships*, Kay Douglas writes,

> *"Unacknowledged fears play on our minds and sap our confidence until we have no energy left to deal with the problems at hand. The way out of fear is through it." She goes on to say, "As we face and feel our vulnerability, our fear may increase in intensity for a brief time. Then it begins to diminish. When we know what we are dealing with much of the power of that feeling goes. We move through fear to a calmer, stronger place within. Having faced the worst, we are free to put our energy into coping creatively with our situation."*[2]

It's Time to Make the Right Choices

You do not deserve to be abused, nor are you to blame for the abuse that you have suffered. Abuse of any type is wrong. If you are in an abusive situation, the first step toward new life and freedom is to recognize that there is a need for a change in your life. Change can be difficult, and in some cases—frightening. However, in any type of an abusive situation, change is absolutely necessary for your own well-being.

Remember, abuse is about power and control. You may be experiencing verbal or emotional abuse now. But if changes are not made to resolve your current situation, then when your husband begins feeling as if he still does not have enough control, the abuse will escalate into more violent forms. According to the Metro Nashville Police Department, Domestic Violence Division, "When abusers hit or break objects or make threats, almost 100 percent resort to physical battering." [3] What might be verbal abuse now could turn into physical abuse down the road. No form of abuse is acceptable!

Contrary to what you may believe, *you are not powerless!* You are a worthwhile person and you do not have to continue to accept your husband's mistreatment. You have the power to make your own choices.

For more information on how to break the cycle of violence in your life,
please order the complete booklet entitled

A Way of Hope

at **1-800-FL-TODAY** (1-800-358-6359) or
at **www.familylife.com**

Notes

1. Lou Brown, Francois Dubau, Merritt McKeon, J.D., *Stop Domestic Violence—An Action Plan for Saving Lives* (St. Martin's Griffin, 1997), p. xiii.
2. Kay Douglas, *Invisible Wounds—A Self-Help Guide for Women in Destructive Relationships* (Penguin Books, New Zealand, 1996), p. 176.
3. Quoted by permission from material provided by the Metro Nashville Police Department, Domestic Violence Division.

Loving Your Military Man
 First edition 2007

13 12 11 10 09 08 07   10 9 8 7 6 5 4 3 2 1

ISBN-13: 978-1-60200-053-7

Printed in the United States.

Senior Editor: Dave Boehi
Editors/Proofreaders: Anne Wooten, Dale Walters and Susan Matthews
Illustration, Cover and Interior Design: Fran Wadkins
Cover Photo: Jenni I. Smith

Dennis Rainey, President
5800 Ranch Drive
Little Rock, Arkansas 72223
1-800-FL-TODAY • www.familylife.com

750 Middle Ground Boulevard
Newport News, VA 23606-2587
1-800-444-6006
www.milmin.org